Sixteen years a child
Sixty years an adult

Bob Cheesman

Sixteen years a child, sixty years an adult

ISBN 978-0-473-45579-8

Contact Email: 16.60.parenting@gmail.com

To our wonderful children and their partners – Martin and Cathy, Janet and Paul, and to our gorgeous granddaughters – Philippa, Emily, Rachael, Isabelle and Madeleine. Thank you for being in our lives.

With much thanks to Mary, my wife of over 50 years for her continual checking and rechecking; to my daughter Janet for sorting my preacher's tautology; Julie Robertson-Steele who corrected my grammar and to Ruth Baker who so wonderfully helped and challenged me. Also to my author friend Barbara Arnold for her encouragement to write and keep writing.

Finally to my editor Jenny Smart for her encouragement, help and patience, and to her husband Richard who undertook the formatting.

Why?

Because children are a gift to be cherished and loved, but they do not remain children, they become adults.

Parenting is about preparing children for adult life and childhood is essential in the development of that adult.

The intention is not to tell you how to parent, but to challenge your thinking so that you can decide as a couple how you will parent.

Introduction

My sister and I were brought up in the Shaftesbury Homes; an institution that looked after orphans and children whose homes were dysfunctional. We were only four and five years of age when we were taken there. We were war children – our father fought during the Second World War but the war affected our parents' marriage severely and they divorced during the war. For reasons never fully understood by us, we were made wards of court. This meant that we were no longer under our parents' guardianship. The Court authorities took that role and they placed us into the care of the Shaftesbury Homes. Consequently, we had little experience of home life but for the occasional school holiday with our father and stepmother. Our mother was not on the scene and I did not meet her until I was eighteen. More often than not, I was sent to foster parents for holidays or stayed at school and rarely saw my father and stepmother. Our daily life was in institutions, not home, and added to that, my sister Pat and I were separated from the age of about seven. We were sent to different schools without any prior warning and hardly saw each other again until we were adults.

Looking back, life felt difficult and often harsh for somebody with my personality. I felt very alone, even though I lived with 300 other boys. I was a shy, introverted child who felt afraid most of the time and this restricted both my learning and capabilities.

There were occasional bursts of light in this darkness but all too often this light was snuffed out. An example of this was the time I was selected to play rugby for the under-fifteen side. I knew nothing of faith in God, yet I began to pray that I might improve my skills and even get onto the school team. I started to jump in the line-out and succeeded in getting the ball back to the scrum half and much to my amazement, was picked for an away match. However, during the match I froze and had to endure much bullying and ridicule on the bus going back to school. I never played for the school team again - I was just too scared.

My childhood was not a good one. When I left school at the age of sixteen I was very ill-equipped for life, let alone getting married and having children. What did I know of parenting when for all of my life I had lived with a bell sounding to tell me to get up, to wash and go to meals, to go to class and eventually to bed, only for it to start all over again the next morning, and all this in an environment where non-conformity meant the cane.

To demonstrate how ill-equipped, I was for life outside the institution, I remember one lunchtime, not long after I had started work, when everyone had gone out and I was left in charge. I was sixteen and had never used a telephone, so when it started ringing I did not have the faintest idea what to do. I had, of course, seen others use the phone, so I picked it up and said very tentatively, "Hello," whereupon a voice said, "Hello," and I replied "Hello." "Hello," he said again and I also replied, "Hello," and then put the phone down. The point I make is that I was not at all prepared for life outside the institution. Life was a struggle – I had to learn how to live in a world where nobody was making decisions for me and I had to take responsibility for myself. For example, clean clothes just arrived each week at the Home and I just left the dirty ones in a pile with all the other boys' clothes. Washing clothes, cooking food, shopping – I had no idea how to go about such things.

There have been three things that changed my life in significant ways. These helped with the fear I lived with and gave me success in life. Darkness became light and I am very grateful for all three.

The first happened in my sixteenth year – just a few months before I was to leave the Home. A film company came to make a promotional film about the Shaftesbury Homes and I was detailed to help the film crew. There were two of us asked to help – I loved it and worked hard with the crew but the other boy used it as an excuse to 'skive off'. I virtually became part of the crew over the two weeks they were filming at the school. At the end of the shoot, and unbeknown to me, the cameraman, Bunny Onions, spoke to the school welfare officer, Commander England, and told him that if I wanted a job he would have one for me. I was thinking of becoming a police cadet but I decided to accept this extraordinary offer.

I started work as a messenger boy and trainee cameraman with the film company and within a few years became a successful rostrum cameraman. I was even head-hunted by another producer when an advertisement I shot won an award at a prestigious film festival.

The second significant thing happened when I was twenty-four. I very reluctantly started going to church – reluctantly because religion was a big part of institutional life and I wanted nothing more to do with it. However, I found myself confronted by the reality of Jesus Christ and became a Christian some time later. This had a huge impact on my life, not only changing me in my inner man but also in the direction I was to walk. Quite unexpectedly the call of God came and I left the film industry and became a full-time pastor of a church in 1978. It has been an absolute privilege to serve God's people ever since.

The third significant thing was getting married to Mary and having our own two wonderful children, Martin and Janet. Parenting was something that we had to work out. The only example I had was boarding school and I knew I did not want our children brought up in that way. Fortunately, Mary came from a stable, loving Christian home with good principles. However, we had no plan on how we were going to parent our children and no idea of what that end goal would be. It was a case of taking each day as it came and hoping it would all work out in the end. We did make it in remarkably good shape, thanks largely to our faith and the goodness of God, and as we followed Biblical principles and watched and learnt from our friends.

Because I wanted our children to have a childhood different from my own, I found myself observing other families and soon began to gain some insight into why some parents were having difficulties. When I became a pastor of a church and others began to consult me, I began to observe parenting styles and think about parenting from different viewpoints. The ideas written in this book are not new but they are the result of nearly fifty years observing and seeking to counsel others.

Whenever I hear of teenagers getting into trouble, doing burn-outs on public roads, driving at high speed from the police, binge drinking, taking drugs or getting into fights, I ask myself how we can help future generations to avoid such lifestyles. Is it the teenagers' problem or is it society's? It seems to me that young people do virtually what they like because we, as a society and parents, have allowed them to.

What if we were to start again? What if we were able to gain an understanding of the issues as parents in such a way that we were able to possibly change the situation for the future? It is a tall ask and I do not claim to be an expert, but simply want to pass on what I have experienced as a parent and what I have observed over the years. I have shared not only my own struggles and mistakes but also what I have observed, both good and bad.

Written here are my thoughts, resulting from those experiences and observations, plus of course, those of my wife and our joint experience of parenting two children, and watching the way they have in turn fostered good standards in their own children.

When a couple approach us to get married, we (with their permission) do quite intensive preparation with them. In recent years we have offered a six-month check-up for newly-weds and every couple has been eager to take up the offer. We have all found this to be very beneficial. However, when couples we have worked with become parents, Mary and I in the past have not discussed parenthood with them. What we have now begun to do is offer teaching about parenting when couples are expecting their first child. This has been well received and so far, proved very beneficial. We also encourage them to do any courses on parenting that are available, and there are some good ones around. This book is an expanded version of what I have been teaching these couples and my prayer is that it will prove helpful to you as well.

I want you to understand that the end result of parenting is adulthood, and to help you gain insight into the steps that bring children to adulthood in good shape to live in our world successfully. It is not intended to be a rule book but a manual; an insight gained through experience and observation. My ideal is that in gaining insight and understanding, you will be better equipped at setting a path for your children to become well-balanced adults. There are, unfortunately, no guarantees, because in the end when our children become adults, they must decide the direction they will take. However, we can seek to give them the best possible start so that they have the potential to make sound judgments.

Part one of this book is for all parents of children under five but would be at its most useful for couples expecting their first child. It is not dealing with baby stuff but with the development of character. You may think this has little relevance in the first months of your child's life. However, it is essential that you understand what is happening to your child during those first months as it affects their future character development. If you understand what is happening, then you will be able to start to set in place the routines needed for successful parenting, and that will help with the seamless transition from baby to toddler and onwards.

This book comes with the hope that you as parents will enjoy the experience of parenting as much as Mary and I have had. Bob Cheesman

Preface

The story you are about to read illustrates why we need to understand how our children grow and learn. What shapes their future lives as adults? What influences them? How does childhood shape their character? How do they develop the skills that enable them to live in the world as adults? What part do we as parents play in the shaping of this future adult? Knowledge allows us to understand and helps us shape our children's character. Ignorance leaves everything to chance.

Jim's story

Some dear friends of ours had a very rough time with their firstborn son – let's call him Jim; not his real name.

This is very difficult to write as I am attempting two things in doing so, both of which can create some difficulties. The first is that I am analysing the situation second-hand. I do not know Jim and did not know his parents during Jim's childhood. This makes it difficult for Jim's parents as I am making assumptions about their parenting, not only in Jim's teen years but also during the years leading up to that period of great difficulty. Were there clues that indicated that there could be difficulties ahead?

As a side note, it needs to be stated that like Mary and I, Jim's parents had no guidance or teaching in parenting. In those days we just had to get on with it. In some things we did all right; in others, we got it wrong. We did not understand what was happening to our children and it had unforeseen consequences. We followed our own childhood experiences and what we saw around us, for good or bad.

The second thing I am seeking to do is look at Jim's story for clues that could help other parents. This is not just a story of the teen years but a look at the whole child to seek to understand any trigger points which would indicate any problems that could evolve later. In doing this I am exposing Jim's parents to a critical view that might cause them some problems. As Mary and I met with them to hear their story we were struck by their fortitude. They were very open and willing to let me probe into, not only their son's behaviour, but also their parenting.

From birth, Jim loved cuddles and was always loved by his parents. Although the family had some very good times with lots of laughter and fun, Jim was a strong-willed, stubborn child who did not sleep well, did not feed well and at times seemed to be angry. Because he had difficulty sleeping he often slept with mum and dad. He also had major temper tantrums and his mum described the time he gave her a look that frightened her. It was very difficult for Jim's parents as he just would not seem to bow to any correction.

Jim's parents freely admit that they indulged him and were not focused or firm enough during those early years. They had the love and commitment to their son but not the discipline or parenting skills needed to guide such a strong-willed and stubborn baby. As with so many of us parents, we take the easy way, mainly because we know no different.

This situation continued throughout the early years and as Jim entered the middle years, Jim's dad joined the army. His parents told me that with hindsight this may have resulted in insecurity for the young Jim.

There appears to have been two sides to the young Jim during the middle years. On the one hand, he excelled academically and began to learn music and had lots of friends. He was also a born joker with a very good sense of humour. However, on the other hand, he also broke into a house during these years causing damage and showed little shame or remorse when caught. Even though he did not do this alone his parents felt that he would have been the instigator. This is one of many things like that. He also began shouting at the devil while at the same time going to church and worshipping God.

What we see is a troubled young lad and his parents did not really know what to do with him. One problem for Jim was that his character was out of kilter; in other words, the combination of character traits in Jim had some anomalies which had not been corrected during the early years, and this often sent him in the wrong direction.

It was during Jim's early teen years that Jim's parents were introduced to the support group 'Tough Love'. This introduced them to other parents who had a child similar to Jim. These parents struggled with the expectations of what was considered normal and needed help as their situations were anything but normal. The 'Tough Love' group helped in bringing some support, understanding and coping strategies to Jim's parents. Through discussion and the suggestions of others in the group, they were enabled to set ground rules for Jim's behaviour within their family unit. The group did help but unfortunately it was too late to make a real difference in shaping Jim's character and behaviour.

As young Jim advanced into his teen years he began to listen to music that led him towards a violent and cruel side of life. He began to write very dark poetry, take drugs and even attempted suicide. Without going into detail, let's just say that things got so bad that at the age of around fifteen or sixteen Jim was removed from his home by Social Services. This was entirely because of his behaviour and actions and in no way caused by his parents. Jim never returned home and went flatting at the age of seventeen or eighteen.

There came a point where Jim's parents realised that every firstborn son on one side of their family seemed to be in trouble of one sort or another. It was as though there was a generational curse on every firstborn male. Jim's parents had another son who was not affected like Jim – in fact, he was the opposite and never caused any real trouble. Such things as generational curses are worth considering. If detected then urgent prayer needs to be sought to break the curse with the help of those who are skilled in dealing with such things.

Jim's parents remained steadfast under extreme pressure while experiencing high anxiety for their son and for their own sanity. Throughout Jim's life, his parents maintained four very important principles that I believe made a big difference to the final outcome for Jim:

- They always loved him unreservedly even when things were at their toughest
- They never rejected him at any stage of his childhood; he was always their beloved son
- They always made physical contact with Jim throughout their shared ordeal
- They always found something to laugh about

The wonderful thing is that Jim is now a wonderful man with a family of his own, very involved with his local church and living a very stable life. He also has a very good relationship with his parent's – he is loved by them and they are very proud of him.

How did this change happen? Through a faithful family member who never gave up on him and eventually led him back to the Lord Jesus. When that happened, he was not only saved but completely restored and now leads a godly stable life in Christ.

What can we learn from this family's experience?

1. We need to learn how to parent and prepare ourselves before our child is born. There are many parenting courses, books and ideas on how to go about parenting. We need to find one that not only makes sense to us and fits our capabilities but also clearly sets us an end goal we can identify with. For me, that end goal is training our children's character so that when they reach adulthood they will be able to stand tall in this world of ours. If that rings your 'parenting bell', then you need to find out all you can that will help you along that path. This book has been written to help you see how you can do that. You then have the end goal and can work out how you are going to go about that task.

2. Pray for your baby at birth, committing him or her to God.
   If there has been sickness or trauma during pregnancy then seek healing for any effects on the baby. Ask God for his or her future as an adult. When somebody who is godly visits in those first few days, get them to pray for your baby asking for the blessing of God on this new life entrusted to your care.

3. Understand that the first five years are crucial in forming good character. During those first five years, you are overwhelmingly the principal guardian, teacher and example for your baby. What Jim needed were parents who understood that they were the ones shaping his character and that they played a crucial role in his development.

4. The middle years are the years where you help consolidate and confirm your child's character traits. The early years are the most important, but the middle years are where those character traits become fully established.

   No matter what, always have faith in God for your child and keep praying throughout their lives. Jim's story is ultimately one of triumph; it was a tough road that has ended well.

Contents

Part One

The Early Years

Chapter 1

Parents

Before we look at parenting itself, let's consider the partnership into which our child is to be born. The relationship between parents can have an advantageous or detrimental effect on our child's welfare, development, confidence and sense of well-being,. not only during childhood but also in their lives as adults.

Understanding this will shape the way you think about your own relationship before, during, and ongoing into the parenting years.

Underlying all good parenting is a loving couple who are committed to each other and who love, protect, cherish, nurture and train their child together for life as an adult. This has an incredibly positive effect on the development of your child's character so that they can stand up in this world with confidence in who they are.

A child is born, usually, but not always, as a cherished valuable addition to a loving couple and is passionately wanted. I realise this when I have seen friends who are unable to conceive. There is a longing for a child which deeply hurts and this passion for a child leaves a very large hole in their lives. I have seen two couples who felt like that and had children after ten years of trying. The joy and tenderness with which their child was welcomed was a wonderful thing to see.

Having considered the passion with which we desire to have children, it will be helpful to understand our importance as parents from our child's perspective. Here is the point – who and what you are has a huge influence on who they will become as adults. It is important to understand how important you are as a couple to the security and well-being of your child during the whole of their childhood and even into adulthood. I would also like to stress the fact that the partnership into which you bring your child is vital to their future view of adult life and future relationships.

I want to enable you to grasp the importance of you both being on the same page when it comes to parenting and realising that consistency and togetherness are vital not only for your child's well-being but yours as well.

To your child, you are, initially, their whole known world. They don't have to think about it, it is inbuilt. They are born into it, they belong and they are at home. They did not ask to come, we as prospective parents asked them to come; they know nothing else. We created our child whether by accident or design. As the saying goes, 'A child does not choose their parents'. Baby is a part of us and our responsibility. As baby grows he or she knows one thing instinctively; that they belong to us, we are mum and dad.

As you grasp the fact that your relationship and example are important, it will make you intentional rather than reactive in your own relationship, and therefore in your parenting.

Being reactive means that you have no plan or understanding in your parenting role so you react to situations as they arise. This can mean that there is no consistency between you as parents and that each parent could react in a different way. The result; lack of consistency and confusion in your child.

Intentionality means being deliberate or purposeful. It means that together you have had a thoughtful discussion about how you are going to go about parenting.

To achieve this consistency you will need to be informed and understand the issues involved. This comes through reading books, talking to grandparents, observing different parenting styles and seeing some of the resulting behaviours in the children around you.

Never forget that you come from two different parenting backgrounds. This makes it imperative that you find agreement in how you are going to approach parenting. The way we were brought up is the example we assimilate and then automatically play out when we have our own child. The problem is that one partner comes from one parenting example while the other may have a very different model. The difficulty is that this can result in confusion in your parenting styles. Baby needs a consistent pattern of parenting so that he or she can be secure, at peace and within an atmosphere which enables their brain to develop and learn as it should.

The second potential problem when partners have different approaches to parenting is a gradual breakdown of communication between you as a couple. A breakdown of communication usually leads to frustration and relationship problems – not a good way to start the parenting journey, especially when you consider how important your relationship is to your baby. Yet it is not only about the baby; your relationship is also important. You need the love, support and security you give to each other. Just for a moment, jump ahead to when your new baby leaves home; how will you be as a couple? Still in a loving relationship with each other? In order to achieve this, you need to maintain your relationship right now, even with this new life to consider. For this reason, you would be advised to explore the issues prior to baby's arrival because you both have to be on the same page or your baby and yourselves will be confused. Both of you will instinctively approach parenting based on your own experience as a child unless you set a time to come together and intentionally set out a plan to develop a united approach to your parenting.

There is a principle running right through this book that is 'what you are your children will become'. Children emulate what they see; how parents behave themselves with each other, with relations and friends – this is the standard they are most likely to absorb. Their example will be what they are being shown by their parents and relatives. Do you shout and swear at each other? Do you have bad habits like drinking too much, gambling, lying and smoking? Are you running down and negatively gossiping about relatives, your boss or what about disrespectfulness, selfishness, manipulation, anger or laziness? What effect does your general conversation in front of the children teach them about how to conduct themselves in regard to others? These are negative and character corrupting.

Love, respect, affection, serving, caring and supporting one another are positive character attributes that will directly affect your child's character positively.

Memories we make as a family also have a huge influence in the development of our child. What will your child remember about their childhood that will shape the interests they have as adults? What will you do as a family that will pull you together and establish those important childhood memories that affect their interests in their future adult lives?

Are you an outdoor adventurous couple who are always up to something? Do you love sport, art, culture and reading or do you sit and watch TV, soaps or play games all the time? It is not that these do not have their place but it is understanding that what you are sparks your child's interests. This book will stimulate your thinking in these areas.

If you are to be a single parent the same principles apply to you, although you are on your own. It is much more difficult to parent single-handed. Who you are is very important to the development of your child. The same principles addressed in this chapter also apply to you. I have had the privilege of knowing quite a few single parent families and have seen many of those children reach adulthood. Many have done a very good job at parenting and their children are great people and a testament to their parent. If you are to be or are a single parent, then the support of wider family, church and friends is very important. I well remember one young man who developed a strong mentoring relationship with the man of a childless couple during his teen years. This was very fruitful for him and a great blessing to his mum. See chapter two titled 'Whanau'.

The relationship between parents needs to be maintained before, during and after the birth of their child. Having a baby affects the balance of the relationship between parents because new mum is passionately focused on the baby. She, much more than new dad, may often feel very tired and emotional. She needs a partner who will be there for her, serving and expressing love in word and deed, especially in the first few months. During this period this is the male partner's role – love, support and help for both new mum and baby. It is not just practical help, like looking after the baby for a few hours to give mum some 'me' time but making a fuss in whatever way blesses his partner - flowers, chocolates, notes expressing love and support, little touches that make new mum believe she is more than a sleep-deprived feeding machine. It is a singularly unselfish role of giving without much receiving.

However, our new dad does need to know he is loved and appreciated, not taken for granted and is not taking third place behind the new baby. After all, baby belongs to both parents.

There comes a time for returning to work for one, or in some cases, both new parents. However, the hope is that mum, who in today's world often has to work as well to adequately provide for the family, has as much parental leave as possible to spend with baby during those first crucial months. Usually it is dad who goes back to work first and in this case, it is his partner's role to make sure he has enough sleep and freedom to fulfil that obligation. Of course, there are many variations with grandparents and childminders often in the mix if both parents are required to return to work. If this is the case, joint responsibility to share the load in the early months is vital to the family's well-being.

There comes a point in time where the restoration and development of the parents' relationship needs to be fully re-established. A new norm emerges; a family norm rather than the one you had as a couple. A good parental relationship brings great security to your child and points the way for their own secure future.

To fulfil this takes love – but love is not just having a feeling; it is being fully committed to give baby a secure base in which to grow, expand and flourish. It is a beautiful thing to love.

When the going gets tough

In today's society, there are many ways in which partnerships are formed. It is when children arrive and a couple becomes a family that it can become difficult. Then, with a possible relationship break down and the change of circumstances that a child brings, separation can result.

Ask yourself; what is the effect on children when parents suddenly announce that they are separating? Don't confuse this with losing a parent from illness, accident or war, even though that is devastating.

Separation means that both parents are going to live in different places and yet are still around. One parent is deliberately separating and moving out.

Consider the problem from the child's viewpoint. Living with mum and dad is their whole known world. It is their life, their security, their safe place, where they belong. It is not the house or district, but being with mum and dad. Suddenly they have two homes and each of their parents potentially has another person living with them. What is it like to live like that, two homes with time split between the two? Rather than creating security, it must create insecurity and uncertainty; rather than contentment, it must create mental turmoil.

The best place for children to flourish, develop and learn is undoubtedly with the mother and father to whom they were born. Why? Because children need love, stability, security, protection and both mental and physical nourishment in order to have the best chance of becoming stable adults in our world.

(It has to be pointed out that if the relationship between mum and dad is mentally abusive, violent or unfaithfulness is present, the children are also going to suffer as a consequence. There are circumstances where one of the parents has no choice but to separate. And yes, this is sometimes the better option for the children.)

In December 2016 the BBC showed a documentary called, Mum and Dad are splitting up. This documentary portrayed the deep hurt children feel when their parents split up. This hurt is not a short-term effect that goes away when the separation is all finalised and the dust has settled. It burns deep and can create long-term behavioural and emotional problems. It would seem that some parents are more concerned for themselves and do not realise the impact it will have on their children if they split up. (Use the link at the end of this chapter to view an article in the *Daily Mail* on this programme (1) or watch the programme itself at: https://vimeo.com/72560382

As a result of the separation of parents, one-third of children in the UK live with only one parent.[1]

I come from a separated family. I cannot remember my parent's separation as I was very young. However, I can tell you the long-term effect it has had on me. I lived with a sense of isolation, of not belonging anywhere. It was like there were big gaps that could not be filled by anything around me. There was, in effect, missing content in my past that could not be recovered, and yet deep within me was this desire to be in contact with my parents, to be a part of their lives and the life of my sister – to belong.

Of course, the pain of separation is also felt by the parents and sadly too often the hurt causing this separation is too severe to be reversed. This

---

1 http://www.dailymail.co.uk/femail/article-2411830/What-divorce-really-does-children--shattering-words-If-youre-divorced-thinking-testimony-shake-core.html (13/12/2016)

offers us a clue as to how many relationships could be saved. Basically, it starts with small areas of neglect that fester until there is an eruption.

Is there hope, is it possible to avoid the breakdown of relationships and therefore avoid the trauma separation brings to our children?

In considering this it reminds me of Mary and I during the first ten years of our marriage. It was a rough time for Mary and I, and I believe we could easily have separated. Recently I heard somebody say, "If only partners would stay together it often comes right in the end." This was true for us – we realised that we were ignorant of how to build a good partnership together so we read and worked at it, and it came right for us. Our marriage vows played a great part in our staying together. We had made promises to each other that we would not only love and cherish each other but also that we would also remain true to each other until death separated us. Those promises were real and needed to be remembered – they reminded us that we were committed to each other. That, of course, was not enough; we also needed to commit to understanding what was happening and correct what was going wrong with the way we were treating each other. We did this by reading, talking to people we trusted and sought to understand what the Bible said about marriage. For me, having been brought up in institutions, I discovered that I was looking for my wife to act like a mother to me. Because I had never lived at home with mum and dad this was a basic instinct but it was not good for our marriage relationship. I had to lay that aside and become a husband. I had to work at being the best husband I could be and, of course, that meant understanding what a husband was. I found out what the Bible had to say on the matter. What did I find? That I should love Mary as I loved myself; in effect, that I should give myself up for her.[2] It is amazing the effect unselfishness has! Mary also responded to what the Bible had to say to her, that she should love and respect me. Gradually we began to heal our relationship and our marriage became stronger and stronger. Another powerful revelation that helped us both was the realisation that men and women are different. They think differently and act things out differently. They are equal but different.

---

2 Ephesians 5:25-33

One powerful incentive for me was that I hated what the alternatives were for our children, and I hated what separation would do to them and Mary. From the beginning, I was determined that I would remain faithful to Mary, to the promises I had made her, and to our children. Never for one moment did we consider separation, even in the darkest time of our marriage. I had the opportunity to be unfaithful; it was very tempting and would have been very easy, but at what cost to my wife and children? At the time of writing this, we are three days away from our fifty-first wedding anniversary and it is not a case of grinning and bearing it. We now have a genuine loving partnership and are a great source of pride to our children. We could have given in, but instead we sought help, read many books on the subject, kept our vows to each other and as a result our children had a stable partnership to which they belonged.

The secret, then, is dealing with the small areas and not letting them fester until they become a boil that could burst and become very messy.

All this came home to me when I preached in a church where I was unknown – a friend had recommended me to them. After the meeting, a man approached me for help as he was having serious marriage problems and was thinking of leaving his wife. They had school-age children. As he told me his story I realised that I had to speak quite strongly to him or he would continue down the road of separation. As the story unfolded I could see what he was blind to. His wife had suffered a family trauma and this had had a deep effect on her, making her withdraw into herself. He thought she was just being difficult and needed to just 'snap out of it'. I knew this would be my only chance to make a real difference to this situation as I lived some distance away. I explained what it was I was seeing and told him I thought his wife needed him. I asked, "What did you promise her when you married?" He told me that he had promised to love her for their entire lives, for better or for worse, in sickness or in health. My candid advice to him was, "Keep those promises, go and love your wife, give yourself up for her. Buy her some flowers on the way home and tell her you are sorry and continue to love her right through her pain." The problem was that he was only looking at his own problems, how that made him feel, and how his wife was not supporting him. He was not giving himself to her when she was suffering; he had forgotten his promise to love her for better or worse, in sickness or in health. I had a ten-minute conversation to try and turn his eyes toward his wife, and then I was gone.

Some months later he came to stay with a friend close to where I lived and I met him in church one Sunday morning. He gave me a hug and told me he had not liked my advice one bit but it had saved his marriage. He had taken my advice and his wife had responded to his love. However, I had not saved his marriage; he had. I had simply reminded him of what he had promised her. He responded and he saved his marriage. I was very glad for him and his wife, but I rejoiced that his children had been saved from the trauma of separation.

It is great to have children – I love mine so much it hurts sometimes. I love my grandchildren with the same passion. Through it all Mary and I have increased in love and commitment for each other. Our children did not separate us; they are and always will be a part of us both.

Chapter 2

Whanau

If you are a New Zealander you will recognise and understand the Māori term 'whanau' (pronounced ˈfɑːnaʊ'). Whanau means family and includes extended family. It is much more than the Western World's linear family, which leans toward thinking of mum, dad and the children as being an independent unit. Others, of course can pop in and out when requested but any input is not welcome unless asked for. The concept of whanau is deeply seated in Maori culture and seems to have many levels, which encompasses the wider community, or even the tribe, in a commitment and loyalty to one another.

In my early days as a pastor in the inner city of London, there were places (before the slum clearances) where generations of families were born, lived and died. Often up to three generations lived in the same house or nearby streets – family, siblings, aunts and uncles all living in close proximity. When a couple married and had children they would become part of this wide supporting family. This sounds wonderful in principle because underlying it all was a rich sense of community and collective responsibility. (It must be noted that there were many problems in these communities as well, and it could sometimes be frustrating and overbearing if there was too much unwanted interference.) New parents would be encompassed in this strong culture with its strong standards of behaviour and respect built into it. There was a wealth of experience and support available to new parents. People used to tell me that doors were never locked and that parents could just pop around to family members and leave the baby there for a couple of hours, in a way which seems impossible now.

With the break-up of this close-knit community where generations lived close by, we have moved into a more linear lifestyle - progressing from one stage to another in a series of steps that separate us from wider family influences. We live at home as a child, then move out to university or single life, then maybe get married and have children. Sounds normal, but entrenched into this is the tendency towards independence and separation from readily available family support, encouragement and help. In other words, we now largely live with little of the family support that past generations had. Whether this is good or bad depends on many things. Good parents who are now grandparents can pass on their experience to the new parents. The new parents can then feed on that experience, keep what is good and gently reject what is not felt to be in keeping with their own jointly worked out parenting style. It is essential that you are united in your parenting principles when grandparents and family become involved.

A couple asked me for advice when one of their grandmothers strongly objected to the discipline style they had chosen to use for their child. Grandma was far too strong in her opinions and it brought much confusion to these young parents. They had decided to follow a certain course but grandma insisted that they follow her way, (which they strongly disagreed with), so much so that they had to sit down with her and confront the issue. Unfortunately, grandma's insistence that she was right almost led to a breakdown in their relationship. Eventually, she did give way and accepted that the parents were not going to change their parenting style, and in the end became a very helpful and loved grandma. As the parents, you need to be united in what you have decided and communicate that with grandparents, asking them to support and help you, thus avoiding confusion and inconsistency.

Conversely, over the years I have heard many grandparents say that they are not allowed to interfere in any way with their grandchildren's lives. They are not allowed to correct, direct or give input. This can be a great disadvantage for new parents as grandparents have so much experience and help to bring.

Mary and I have been very fortunate in that we have always been encouraged to do all of these things with all of our five grandchildren. This has been a great privilege. However, this honour must not be abused as there are unwritten conventions that need to be kept. This was true even in those large extended families in the inner city of London where I worked. As new parents, it is important that you not only read books such as this but also ask future grandparents what they think. Get as much advice as you can, but having got advice make up your minds as to your parenting plan. Grandparents need to respect how you have decided to go about parenting, even if they are set in ways that you do not agree with.

Express your views, explain your reasons, ask them to 'be on the same parenting page' and allow them to help you. In this way, you are bringing the experience of two families together and taking the best from both. These same principles also apply to aunts, uncles and friends who babysit. An example of this for us were rules around eating. We had rules that our daughter did not like when growing up, so she and her husband went about it in a different way. We needed to adhere to her rules when we had the grandchildren over for sleepovers at our house. This was good because her way was not wrong, just different. If we had thought she was wrong we may have asked her why she was doing it that way or suggested something different, but it would not have been right for us to blatantly ignore her and her husband's rules for their children.

Grandparents can be a great sounding board. One night our daughter was having trouble getting her firstborn to sleep. She had been up most of the night, was very frustrated and did not know what to do. She thought she could not ring anyone as it was in the early hours of the morning. She then remembered that she was in New Zealand and we were in England so for us it was daytime, so she rang and chatted around the issues and felt much better and more able to cope.

One of the great joys of being a grandparent is that it is okay to spoil the grandchildren; in fact, I often say it is a grandparent's right. As new parents, this can be confusing at first and I guarantee that the time will come when you will say something like, "You would never have done that when I was a child." This is because grandparents do not have the same responsibility as you, the parents. This leads to a favourite saying of grandparents – 'Thank goodness we can give them back'. However, this spoiling should always be under the watchful eye of the parents and should never mean that the parents' views can be overridden. For instance, grandparents are over for Sunday lunch and the children are pestering granddad because they know he has sweets in his pocket. Granddad gets them out but mum calls out, "Not before lunch, Granddad." What should happen at that moment is that granddad should speak up in support of mum. "Mum says no, so we will put them away until mum says you can have them." If granddad does not do this but gives the sweets to the children in spite of mum's instruction, then as parents you need to sit down and have a chat with granddad. Spoiling that overrides parental authority cannot be allowed to continue. I love being a grandparent and love to spoil my grandchildren with treats but you will also find me asking mum or dad, “Is that okay with you?”

The concept of whanau or extended family is very important in the upbringing of children as it supports, helps and underpins you as a family. Actively maintain your relationship, avoid hibernating, and get out amongst your wider family with the baby as soon as possible.

Chapter 3

Where it begins

The desire to have children is strong and when a couple get together they inevitably begin to think of starting a family.

When there are just the two of you, you are a couple. When children are added you become a family. You then become parents who have the responsibility of bringing up your children. Interestingly, one of the definitions of the word 'parent' is 'guardian'. That is 'those who look after, protect and defend somebody who cannot do that for themselves', and without doubt that is true of our children.

I know from my own experience just how wonderful it is to have children. I can also remember what that responsibility felt like and that I was very ill-equipped for that task. What we all have is our own experience as a starting point. The experience of being a child can be a good experience and therefore beneficial, or it can be anything from a bad to a very bad experience. My experience was not family life but boarding school; very different and not a good starting point. We all come to parenthood from different families and backgrounds. Those families may not be in agreement as to how to go about this task of parenting. This will mean that potentially, we as new parents do not have the same ideas, principles or standards when it comes to bringing up children.

My passion is not to tell you how to parent but rather to spark your thinking – hopefully helping you get to a point where together, you as a couple, agree on the parenting principles you will practice in the first sixteen years of your child's life.

For children, family is a place of love where life skills are learnt. Parents have the task of preparing their children for adult life. There are others in the wider family with varying levels of authority, for instance; grandmothers and grandfathers, aunts and uncles, and let's not forget that there may also be brothers and sisters. In addition, there are those to whom the parents delegate the care of their child while they go out to work. However, the primary initial authority for the teaching of life skills lies with the mother and father.

Putting it like that can sound awfully dry and task-orientated, but the reality is that it should never be like that, because the motivating power and atmosphere of family life is and must be love. Without love children just will not flourish. Love generates security, safety, fun and laughter, and above all a sense of belonging.

Your child arrives into this world from within the mother, where he or she has developed through the union of the mother and father. For this reason, this new human being has inherited a combination of their traits and is a unique new personality whose experiences at the time of arrival have all been within the mother. He or she has experienced her heartbeat, her voice and the voice of the father as he has spoken, not only to the growing unseen child but also as he has had conversations with the mother. For many this is a wonderful time, but for others it is difficult. Many are single parents, others are in abusive relationships and for others their children will be adopted at birth.

'At sixteen weeks the unborn child shies away from light: at twenty weeks there is a response to speech patterns: at twenty-five weeks a baby can kick in time to music and at six months the unborn child can understand the subtle shifts in its mother's emotions.'[3]

Consider then what part stress, arguments, anxiety, peace, joy and kindness have to do with a child's experience while in the womb. If the new arrival can pick up the subtle shifts of the mother's emotions, some of those emotions will have a positive effect while others may create a negative effect. Each of these can affect the child's own sense of normality. If peace and joy were the predominant experience while in the womb, then on arrival the child is more likely to exhibit those attributes and be at peace. However, if the experience was mainly stress and anxiety, could it be that when he or she arrives, stress and anxiety are the predominant characteristics that the child demonstrates? Baby may be fretful and lack

---

3 Brain rules for baby. John Medina

peace, always wanting to cling, or demonstrate an inherent fear. Children find it difficult to flourish in life when they are distracted by stress, sleeplessness and anxiety. If this is the case they need to experience the opposite after they arrive – peace, joy and love.

This wonderful gift arrives! Parents have dwelt over names and dreamed dreams of joyful love and emotion. Yet all too often, in the midst of that love there is discouragement and sometimes even despair, made worse by sleepless nights. A new personality has entered the home, one that knows nothing of life outside the womb. Entering this strange environment, they know their mum and dad's voices, their mum's smell; they know how to suck in food, dispel poo and quickly learn that a cry brings the one person they want to stay close to; mum. Bonding with mum and dad is very important to a new-born; it brings security and contentment. Cuddles, time spent looking at you, and listening to you talk to them, combine to strengthen the bonds between parents and child in this new world outside of the womb. Each of these brings security to your new-born child and aids in their brain development.

What do they know of this strange world outside the womb?

Do they understand right from wrong? Do they know how to eat, talk or walk, say 'please' and 'thank you' and relate to other people? Do they recognise grandparents or know how to say 'Hello Grandad' or 'Hello Grandma?' No, of course they don't. Yet they have an amazing, incredible ability to learn and this they do immediately after birth.

How and from whom do they learn all these things? This is the subject of this book. If we understand this, then our child has a great chance of reaching adulthood in good shape and well able to face the world as an adult. So often we think it happens all by itself and we just hope for the best. When Mary and I became parents, I had never had a normal home life with a mum and dad but Mary did, and that was great, but we still did not really understand how to go about being parents. For me, it was about observation. I watched others and decided what I liked and what I did not like. We developed a sense of what we wanted for our children, and how we wanted them to be as adults.

There is also one thing that I determined to do and that was to pray to God for them throughout their whole lives; to pray for them at each stage of their life, and to continue to pray for them when they became adults and eventually started their own families. The same goes for their children. We have prayed for them from the moment they were born. We pray because we want God to bless them in life, not just as children but as adults. We pray they will have wisdom to see and understand what is happening around them. We pray for protection and that they will be of good heart and do good to those they come into contact with. We pray for ourselves that we will do what is right and not frustrate them. We pray that we will help them develop a good personality. Today, when I have the privilege of holding a new-born child in my arms my first thought is, 'What will this child be like as an adult?' I love to pray for them and sense in God what is before them.

Our child has arrived in our family and we are the parents who will guide them to adulthood, to be able to stand up in this world and be well equipped for what is before them. We need to open our minds to understand what is about to happen, for understanding will enable us to enjoy the experience of parenting, and to also endure it when necessary because we understand the goal.

Understanding how the brain develops will help us in this quest. It would seem that the brain of a new-born baby has little information installed, so all our child's information of how to conduct themselves in life and skills has to be installed over the next eighteen to twenty years. How the brain does this is fascinating, but not being a scientist, I can only share my limited understanding. There is a lot of information on the Web so if you wish to explore further you will have no trouble doing so.

The brain forms what are known as 'neural pathways'. The best way to describe these is that when a piece of information or an experience is recorded in the brain it forms a strand of something similar to cotton; very fragile and therefore easily broken, not set. The more information on the same subject or experience that enters the brain reinforces that strand of cotton until it thickens into something similar to string. This can still be broken but not as easily. This continues until it becomes like a steel cable, and therefore extremely difficult to break. It is this same principle that creates addiction to drugs, nicotine and alcohol, and why it is so difficult to break these addictions. Your understanding of this developmental process of the brain will help you understand the following chapters. In reality, the Bible has already explained this in the proverb, 'Train a child in the way he should go, and when he is old he will not turn from it'. (Proverbs 22:6). We will explore this proverb in Chapter six.

Chapter 4

Essential elements

If our children are to flourish in childhood and be fully equipped for adult life, there are certain essentials that are necessary from birth to adulthood.

As a whole, these essentials come under the heading of love. Without love, we shrivel and our growth is stunted. Love is not a push-over. Love that says every whim must be granted is not love, but indulgence. There was a mother of a massively obese young teenager who was so big that he was in serious danger of health problems that would considerably shorten his life. When asked why she had allowed him to get to this point, her reply was, "I love him so much that I can't refuse him anything." That is not love but indulgence, and harms rather than benefits. Love builds up and in a parenting context gives confidence, protection, safety and direction.

We can identify love in three ways:

1. Passionate, sentimental kind of love

This is the touchy, feeling kind – a cuddle, a reaching out and touching, the ruffling of hair, holding our child's hand, sitting and just looking at this wonderful child, wondering at how she or he could come from us. I used to love laying my new-born children, then grandchildren, on my knees, just looking at them, and then later sitting them on my lap, cuddling up reading a book. It was a bit of a shock when one of my granddaughters refused to sit on my lap but wanted to sit next to me when it was story time!

2. Love which develops the companionship and enjoyment of somebody's company

In parenting terms, this is talking and doing things together. 'Making memories' is an expression often used today – going on holiday, taking walks or doing projects together. One of my granddaughters loves projects and we work away in the garage making something from whatever she can find. We have made picture frames, carved her initials out of bits of wood she has found and made a wind-powered car for a school project. This was followed the following year by a solar-powered car – great fun for me as well as her. This kind of love includes the child and develops a companionship that makes them feel secure and lasts a lifetime.

3. Love that looks for a way to be constructive

This love is not possessive nor is it anxious to impress, and it does not have inflated ideas of its own importance. It is an unconditional commitment to the welfare of others and therefore, in this context, to our children. It bears the load, takes appropriate action, supports, develops and guards, and is unconditional and permanent in its commitment and consistent in its behaviour. This is the love which guides, corrects, helps and will not give up.

Love has elements which are essential in developing our children for adult life. Without them emotional and educational growth can become stunted and leave our children emotionally unstable.

Love is made up of the following elements:

Praise

Praise is expressing warm approval or admiration. In a programme broadcast many years ago, a boy was labelled 'the naughtiest boy in England'. He was a handful and the programme focussed on how some psychologists changed that boy's life. One of the issues was negative disapproval under the guise of positive praise. Let me explain – the boy made a house out of Lego and showed it to his parents. They, in turn, admired it and said, "What a lovely house, but where are the windows?" This is something we all do but the reality is that if such negative add-ons are always there, then nothing is ever right. Regardless of the positive opening praise, the negative is always remembered above the positive. As adults we have a perception of how things should be but children under five have no such norms to go by, so we must not expect them to do things as we would. We have all seen a child draw something and then tell us what it is. Does it look like they describe? We must make the positive stand out and be careful of negative input. Negative comments suppress creativity. Genuine praise builds up rather than points out deficiencies.

There is a time for correction, as you will see, but to build up confidence we need praise without any negative add-ons.

Encouragement

This is giving confidence or hope by stimulating development. It is, of course, similar to praise but has the added emphasis on helping children develop in life and gain skills in particular areas. The idea is to build up and encourage forward motion. Let's go back to the Lego house with no windows. How could the boy's parents have stimulated development? They could, at another time, have said, "Let's draw a house; now what are the things that make a house?" They would probably have ended up with a list that included walls, roof, a door and some windows. So, in a positive way, they would encourage development from the house with no windows.

It is also important to understand how the brain develops. If you continually tell a child they are very good, even a genius in what they are doing, it develops within the brain as 'I do not need to try very hard because I am just good'. The result is that over time they will stop trying but rest in the fact they are a genius and do not need to try very hard. If, on the other hand, we praise the effort by saying, "That's a great Lego house you have made, you must have put a lot of effort into that," you are establishing the principle that success comes through effort. This applies right through everyday life, not only in education, individual play or art but in how our children relate to other children and adults. We need to encourage them to share, to say 'hello', to visitors, to say 'please', and 'thank you', and to praise them when they get it right, telling them, "Your manners were so good today, you made a lot of effort to be polite." Keep it as positive as possible. The negative should only come in when they dig their heels in, which I can promise you, on occasions they will. Even then we need to be patient and persistent but should always, if possible, end with praise.

Understanding

One of the meanings of the word 'understanding' is to have 'sympathetic awareness' or 'tolerance'. We will discover that our child already has his or her own personality which may be different from our own. We may be a touchy-feely sort of person, introvert or extrovert but our child may be the opposite. We are not all extroverts or all introverts. We do not all love sport – some love to read, others are artistic, some are practical while others love solitude, and some hate being on their own. We, as parents, need to consciously work at recognising personality traits in our child and accepting them, although a different personality is no excuse for rudeness or impolite behaviour. As our child develops, we can try to have a sympathetic awareness and tolerate the differences in their disposition without tolerating bad behaviour.

Listening

From the earliest age, we should encourage our children to talk to us. However, when they talk we have to make sure we listen and take them seriously. We can begin by talking to them while still in the womb and continue to do so after they are born. Tell them about lots of ordinary things that are going on all around them. It will help their language skills and they will become more aware. I remember an occasion when we were out with our son and his wife and our oldest granddaughter, then a baby. She was in a sling facing her mother and was constantly grizzling. Even at that age mum needed to listen and try to understand why her young daughter was grizzling. Her mum turned her around so that she could see what was going on and the result was immediate. Her eyes roved everywhere looking from one of us to the other as we spoke. All she wanted was to be part of the action. Describe what is going on around the child and then, when they learn to express themselves, it will be quite natural for them to have conversations with us. However, remember to really listen and never ignore what they have to say.

Communicating

The dictionary tells us that to communicate is to 'impart knowledge by speech, writing and gestures'.

Communicating is not lecturing but using everyday events to teach children what is happening around them. Talk, talk, talk! Don't hide subjects away. It is entirely natural for a child to ask why things are like they are. On the other hand, do not make a huge deal out of everything – keep it natural. Remember that there is a developing brain behind the 'why' question. The brain is seeking to file information in its quest to develop, understand and apply concepts. The brain is not like a computer which stores facts that can be recalled exactly as they were imputed. This kind of information gathering could be called flat or one-dimensional. The brain is predisposed to look at information from a multi-dimensional view. It wants to understand the information and be able to apply it to life situations; if necessary from several different perspectives. Our child's new brain seems to achieve this by gradually building up the required information little by little and through repetition. This then is what is happening behind the 'why' questions.

We should never assume our child does not understand what we are saying or what is going on around them. Parents talk in front of their children believing that they do not understand because they are not talking yet. It is my observation that children understand much more than they can express. I have even known parents who say that there is no point in teaching their children anything until the age of five as they cannot possibly understand until then. They say, "... then we will start to train them." Too late I say. Ask any primary teacher and they will tell you that they can tell which children have been trained in everyday life, character-building attributes and those who have not.

Fun

In the period from birth to age five, there should be lots of fun and laughter. Being under five is a carefree time of life where there is no responsibility to provide food or to pay the rent, to learn to read, write, do maths, or play music or sport in any serious way. It is the parents' responsibility to provide protection, sustenance, safety and direction, while the child enjoys the security provided by these things. We, as parents, train our child for life as an adult, but at this age it is about character building, and it must never be so foreboding, harsh or strict, that there is no fun. Our love needs to be full of praise, encouragement and understanding, as we train our child using lots of fun to be the best person they can be.

Chapter 5

Sleep patterns

Sleep is essential to the well-being of our children. Consider what we are like when we are tired. If you are anything like me, you not only find it difficult to concentrate and think things through, but also find it hard to learn and take things in with any accuracy. Tiredness can also make us irritable with those around us and not very pleasant company. Now transfer those thoughts to the under-five-year-old child. A newborn sleeps most of the day at first, but as they become more aware and their brains and bodies develop, they gradually spend more time awake. However, a twelve-month-year-old still needs twelve hours a night plus one or two sleeps in the day.

Let's consider for a moment why they need so much sleep. Their brains and bodies are developing at an astonishing rate, so much so that between twelve and fifteen months they are already walking and beginning to verbally express themselves. This takes a lot of energy for a small body and a developing mind, and the human body needs sleep to renew the energy expended. It is similar to when we have had a hard day's work and need sleep to refresh our body's energy levels – we come home, sit in an armchair and the next minute we are asleep! This is because our body is worn out and needs sleep to regenerate. Even most adults need an average of eight hours sleep a night in order to keep their energy levels up. If lack of sleep is detrimental to us, it is even more so for our infant children. We have all seen a child who is so obviously tired that all they can do is cling to their mum and cry every time she tries to put them down. Their eyes are puffy and red and there is just no energy in them. I have seen children under five who are not getting enough sleep and the parents tell me, "They just will not go to sleep. We try to put them down but they won't stay in bed. They eventually fall asleep on the floor around the time we are going to bed and only then can we pick them up and put them in bed." Some parents say, "If only I had a child who sleeps like my friend's child, it would be wonderful."

Here is the question – is it the child's problem or the parents' problem?

Consider what happens if it is left to a child to determine when they go to sleep. Not all, but a good number of them will force themselves to stay awake as long as possible. There seems to be an instinct in children to fight sleep, although they are often miserable, irritable and bad tempered. "There you are," some will say, "some children are difficult and others are easy," and yes, this is true to a certain extent. However, let's consider that, difficult or not, it is the parents' responsibility to train their children in good sleeping patterns, whether they are strong-willed or passive.

Some children have medical conditions that make sleep difficult, but in this book, we are looking at the majority of children who do not suffer any such complications.

As I have watched our acquaintances' young children I have observed that those who are deprived of sleep are irritable, clingy and prone to tantrums and excessive crying. Those who sleep well are generally well behaved, happy and able to occupy themselves. Currently we have friends who have two young children who both sleep through the night and they are a pleasure to be with. It is also important that our children sleep well for our own sanity because we need time without the interruption of children all evening. It also helps us to function the next day at work or at home with the children. If we are tired and our children are tired it doesn't make for a very peaceful family life. Thus, it is crucial that we establish good sleep patterns in our children as early as possible and be consistent in our bedtime routines.

- Can we train our children to sleep?
- If so, how do we go about it?

Before Mary and I had children, we visited some relatives who had a child of about two. We had a great time saying good night with lots of stories and cuddles before the child was taken upstairs and put to bed. Some minutes later she came back downstairs. She was put back to bed again but she soon came back down. This went on for a while until mum and dad turned to us and said, "What can we do? She will just not stay in bed." Unfortunately, she was then allowed to stay up until everybody went to bed. What was happening here was that the child was dictating her sleep patterns and the parents were giving in to her wishes. At the end of our visit we resolved that this was never going to happen with our children, and it never did. We instilled in them that they did not get out of bed without permission, so much so that the day came when we had to tell them that they were now old enough to get up when they wanted to! Why was it like this with our children? Was it because they were good children? I think it was because we wanted our children to know that bedtime was for sleep and that sleep was essential for well-being, so we expected them to go to bed and stay there, and because we expected that, they followed. It started with us being in control and not allowing that control to be transferred to our children. In these early years, it is essential that we as parents are in control for the good of our children, and this definitely applies with regard to sleep.

In different cultures there are different expectations and patterns, and we must begin to set the pattern that is acceptable in our own culture. The pattern for sleep in our Western culture is that we have our own beds and we go to sleep on our own, and if we wake up then we put ourselves back to sleep. Initially, we have a bassinet in which the baby sleeps which is usually in the parent's room. The baby then transfers to a cot and this is usually in their own room. Eventually they go into their own bed, with the hope that they will sleep well for the rest of their lives.

It is unwise to just 'plonk' our newborn baby into a bassinet and expect that they will sleep instantly all night. That is unreasonable and it just will not happen. They need the comfort and security of parents around them. Remember, they have been in the womb developing for nine months, feeling mum's heartbeat and hearing speech and music. Being near mum and dad is their secure place. However, we can be mindful of the goal and gently introduce the patterns that we want to establish, avoiding unhelpful patterns which will later have to be broken. Our newborn will need night feeding and the comforting cuddles that go with that, for some months after birth.

It is surprising what circumstances dictate. Some friends of ours had a baby daughter named Grace. Grace's parents brought her home from hospital and set up her bassinet, only to discover that their bedroom was so small that they could not get the bassinet in, or if they did, they could not get in and out of bed! They had no choice but to put Grace into her own room next door. They had good bedtime routines – the parents fed her at night and put her back into her own room and if she cried for a little time, they let her, and then she went back to sleep. Within weeks, Grace slept right through the night. Grace had been conditioned that this was the way you went to bed and slept. She learnt that if she cried after being put back to bed, nothing happened immediately, so she learnt to go back to sleep on her own.

So, how do we go about training our children to sleep well?

The first thing we need to grasp is the necessity of setting a right pattern for sleep. Children under five respond and flourish to guidelines or patterns in life; routines. If we set sleep times and keep to those times every day, they will become the norm and baby's brain will begin to signal that at those times it is time for sleep. If consistently applied, this routine becomes a neural pathway in the brain. At those times the brain will signal to baby that it is time to sleep. These patterns of sleep are what we are aiming for with our children and we can begin to set these patterns from birth.

For the first four to six months do not worry about baby sleeping through the night – instead baby's life should centre around feeds, bonding with mum and dad and lots of cuddles so our child feels secure and loved. This time of your life is very tiring and you begin to long for baby to sleep through the night for your own sanity, so when baby is six months old, you could do well to consider training baby to sleep through the night.

There are two opinions as to the best way to train children to sleep – NAP (Night time attachment parenting) and CIO (Cry it out). These are at opposite ends of the spectrum of sleep training and their advocates firmly defend their positions.

1. NAP (Night time attachment parenting)
   NAP is a very infant-driven style of parenting. Baby comes first and is responded to at all times. The idea is to have as much contact with your baby as possible and this means that when it comes to sleep you never leave your baby to cry but respond as quickly as possible.

In general, I wholeheartedly agree with this approach for around the first six months.

2. CIO (Cry it out)

> CIO sleep training comes at a definite point in baby's life when you decide it is time for sleep patterns to transition to sleeping through the night with baby being able to put themselves back to sleep when they wake in the night. CIO is illustrated in the following story:

We have friends in London who used the CIO sleeping routine with each of their five children. For the first six months they established a bedtime routine, (where the child was read to, and then put to bed at the same time each evening) but would be fed and given cuddles if they woke in the night; thus, building a bond of love and security with their child. When their child was six months of age our friends felt that it would better for their child if they could sleep more soundly and stop having night-time drinks so they applied a 'sleep training programme'. The child was put to bed with all the established bedtime routines and left. If the child cried they waited five minutes and then went to see if all was okay. They did not pick the child up or play with them but put the bed clothes back on and said in a firm but loving voice, "It is time for sleep," and left the room. They then waited another twenty minutes before returning and going through the same routine. They repeated this until the child was asleep. This could take up to two hours depending on the child, and they repeated this the next night, and if necessary the third night as well. Not one of their children took more than three nights to learn to put themselves to sleep with little or no protest, and from that moment on, unless they were ill or had teething problems, they slept through the night. None of those children suffered from being left to cry in this way; in fact, it was the opposite, because they then slept well and were much more aware and active during the day.

In contrast to this, other friends of ours learnt this sleep training after three years of spending every evening trying to get their son to sleep and being woken every hour right through the night. They, like lots of parents, hated hearing their child cry and so always gave in and picked the child up for a cuddle and drink. Out of sheer exhaustion they reluctantly applied the sleep training programme, which was much harder to do with a three-year-old, and much to their surprise, it worked.

A variation of this is to time ten minutes between visits rather than twenty as this is slightly easier on the parents' nerves.

I have experience of CIO but the only experience I have of NAP is seeing parents who so dislike hearing their child cry, that they get them up every night when they cry, and that this is still going on when the child is two years of age. When you meet them during the day the parents look worn out and the children are so tired that they cannot respond to anything around them. However, there are parents who just cannot go down the CIO route and the NAP procedure is the best way for them to go.

Is there a right or wrong way to get all children to sleep well? Of course not! However, some paths are easier for both parents and baby, and for my part I am definitely in the CIO camp. Also, there is now research from the Harvard Medical School, to assure us that crying does no harm to our children.[4]

We have to think about what our baby needs and then gently begin to encourage them into routines that reflect the end result we wish to see. It seems to me that babies thrive on routine, so routine needs to be set from birth. We don't need to be hard or rigid about it at first; rather thoughtful and considerate, loving and kind. We often make the mistake of disliking the sound of crying so much that we respond every time by picking our child up. Crying is the only way babies have of expressing themselves. This can be because they are not getting things done their way, or genuine discomfort. One mum told me that, after a while, she could distinguish the different cries of her newborn. Just think; if we got what we wanted every time we yelled we would yell all the time. Children are smart and they have human attributes, one of those being that they want things done their way if at all possible.

The other very important point to understand is that we can condition our child to go to sleep in a certain manner, then blame the child because they will only sleep when the conditions we have created are fulfilled. Have a look at these examples:

Every night Esther goes to bed and mum or dad sit on the bed patting her back until she falls asleep. During the night Esther wakes and cries until mum or dad returns and pats her back until she falls asleep again. Esther

---

4 http://www.health.harvard.edu/blog/new-study-says-okay-let-babies-cry-night-201605319774(6 December 2016)

has been conditioned that the way you go to sleep is being patted, so when she wakes and mum or dad are not there and she is not being patted, she cries until one of them comes and pats her. She then goes back to sleep again.

Tom only goes to bed when mum and dad go, or until he falls asleep on the floor. Whenever mum and dad try to put him to bed he resists by crying until he is allowed to stay up until they go to bed. Tom has been allowed to stay up until he falls asleep of his own accord. For him, this is the only way he has known. His parents have allowed him to dictate his own bedtime.

Pat always goes to bed well. She sleeps at first but then wakes and cries until she is given milk. She is then allowed to sleep in mum and dad's bed. Whenever mum and dad try to put her back into her own bed she just cries until they give up. Pat has been well trained in the bedtime routine and, like all very young children, she needs a night-time feed. However, it is much easier for mum to keep Pat in her bed, so to Pat this is the right way to sleep after her night-time feed.

In each of these examples a pattern was introduced which became the normal way in which the child slept. The pattern was created for the best of reasons but eventually became a real problem for the parents and the child. This was not achieving the required goal of the child learning to sleep through the night and putting themselves back to sleep when they woke.

Parents are the ones who should understand what is best for their children, especially those under five. Sleep is crucial to a child's development and children need to be trained by their parents to get the right amount of sleep. As parents we can make our own decisions about what we think is right for our child, but we need to consider the consequences both for ourselves and for our child. The above examples had considerable consequences for the parents and, what is more, habits were established which were difficult to break.

I learned much of this when consulted by parents whose children had sleeping problems. I began to consider both the attitude of the parents whose children had great difficulty sleeping and those whose children slept well. What I found was the parents whose children slept well were parents who not only expected them to sleep, but also did not allow their children to get up once they had gone to bed. Parents whose children had difficulty sleeping did not seem to have the expectation that it was their bedtime;

full stop. Instead, there was a lack of definite bedtime routines and the parents flowed with the direction their children dictated through protest. This is, of course, a generalisation, with many variations.

I know of a child who went through a very baffling period when he was put to bed after a bath, story time, prayer and kisses. He would just scream when his parents turned the lights out and left the room. They tried everything, until they realised that their son was feeling very insecure and that they needed to solve this in another way. So, when he screamed one of them sat on his bed until he went to sleep. There was no talking, touching, playing or reading because the parents' principles had not changed – when he went to bed he stayed in bed because bed was for sleep. Neither was there the possibility of getting up and coming downstairs, which would have been very convenient and easy. They just sat there with no interaction until he went to sleep. One day they left the room and waited for the screaming but it never came and it never recurred.

Recently, I had the privilege of teaching two couples expecting their first baby how to set good sleeping patterns and routines. Neither of those children concerned have had any real difficulty going to sleep and have slept through the night within weeks of birth. My recommendation is to gently start setting the sleep pattern we want our children to follow right from birth – then when they are six months old apply the principles more firmly. Often the problem comes when it is time to wean children off night-time feeds, so we need to persist.

Part of our sleep training involves getting our children to learn how to put themselves back to sleep when they wake in the night – so we need to be careful not to rush in as soon as they cry in the night, but wait to see if they go back to sleep themselves.

Remember that all this needs to be done within a framework of love, praise, encouragement and understanding

Chapter 6

'Sixteen years a child, sixty years an adult'

Consider for a moment the objective of the whole childhood experience. While it is vital that this period is memorable, fun and fulfilling, it is not the objective. Every child must and does become an adult, so the ultimate objective is adulthood. The reality is that our children will be adults much longer than they are children; hence the phrase, 'Sixteen years a child, sixty years an adult'.

Childhood can be divided into three periods, marked by either starting school or changing schools and each period has a specific objective. The objective of the preschool years is the forming of character. Even though our child is a baby, an important question would be; what sort of adult will they be and what characteristics would we love to see in the adult they will become?

Let's think for a moment about what character is:

'The combination of traits and qualities distinguishing the individual nature of a person; reputation, especially a good one'. (Collins English dictionary)

Character Attributes

This definition of character speaks of reputation, so the question arises as to what we want our child's reputation as an adult to be.

A good reputation might include honesty, integrity, kindness, patience, love, joy, peace, goodness, faithfulness, gentleness, and self-control, while a bad reputation might include anger, hatred, jealousy, unfaithfulness, addictions, and envy.

The objective is to instil good character traits into our new arrival so they will have a good reputation as an adult. Character is not intellectual education. However, developing good character in our child helps to form a basis for future education. A good character enables a child to learn well and not be hindered by negative aspects which characteristics such as anger and jealousy create within them.

Let us consider these three periods of our child's life and what age would be the most important for developing character.

- 0-5 – the preschool years
- 5-11– the junior school years
- 11-18 –the senior school years

Before we consider our choice, we should think about what the major influences in forming good character are in our child. Who is teaching them what is good and what is not so good? Who is correcting and protecting them from danger? It will be different from family to family but we could rate the following influences in our family situations, starting with the most influential. This is not a matter of right or wrong, as different families will have different influences. The idea is to stimulate our thinking beforehand as to how we can develop good character in our child, because the characteristics they will pick up are those of the most influential around them.

0-5 Preschool	**5-11 Junior school**	**11-18 Senior school**
Grandparents	Parents	Parents
Aunties	Friends	Siblings
Parents	Schoolteachers	Peer pressure
Uncles	Grandparents	Teachers
Siblings	Aunties	Advertising
Friends	Uncles	Popular culture/music/TV
Childcare	Siblings	Schoolteachers
Popular culture/music/TV	Peer pressure at school	Grandparents
	Advertising	Aunties
	Popular culture/music/TV	Uncles

What we can understand is that during junior school years, parents' influence begins to lessen and influences from others begin to take effect. By senior school, independence and self-determination begin to take a hold.

Returning to the question posed earlier, 'What is the most important period of our child's life for forming good character?' I would suggest that the 0-5-year period is by far the most important. It is the one period of our child's life when we have more control than any other influences. From the moment they go to school we begin to share this influence with others and by the time they reach senior school, control is being handed over to them bit by bit until they reach an age when they take responsibility for themselves. This is the way it has always been and we cannot fight it, so it is very important that these early years count in forming our child's character. However, we are not dealing with something automatic – our child is a human being and at birth has all the basic characteristics of a human being with an individual disposition.

Some are introverts, others are extroverts; some are shy and others bold. Some are brave and others are timid; some are artistic or academic while others are practical or inventive and still others are musical. There is a great variety in the human race, and what a good thing that is. We cannot and should not expect everyone to be the same – what a boring world that would make. We can produce adults of good character whatever their dispositions. Shyness, as one parent put it to me, is no excuse for rudeness and ignoring people. Our concern here is about building character within the disposition of the child.

So, our child could be:

- Strong-willed or placid
- Introvert or extrovert
- Sensitive or self-willed
- Optimistic or pessimistic
- Dependent or independent

Our children come with the entire gambit of normal human tendencies. Some who are very strong-willed will want us to do things their way and they will fight to get us to conform to what they want. Some parents give in and allow their child to dictate the way things should be done. For instance, some children refuse to go to sleep even when they are ridiculously tired. They want us to cuddle them at all times and feed them whenever they feel like it. Why is that? If we are honest we are like that too. But we have learnt that it is not the way life is and we have to give and receive, to love and to be loved. If we do not learn to give and receive, to be under authority as well as in authority, then as an adult we will struggle. We have also learnt that sleep is vital to human existence and lack of it affects our work and ability to learn. Lack of sleep makes us irritable and not pleasant to live with but our child does not yet know any of this so they have to be taught.

- Every child is unique and special and needs to grow up knowing it
- Every child has their own gifting which will need to be developed
- Every child needs to be loved and to love – to receive affection and to give it
- Every child needs encouragement in order to flourish

Yes, a child develops into an adult – but we cannot make an adult without a childhood, because childhood is what equips them for adulthood.

A family who are well informed and seeking to understand what is happening in their child's development, have the best possibility of seeing their children able to transition into adults who are well equipped for success in adult life.

We all live within cultural expectations. I am writing this in New Zealand where culture has built-in behaviours which are acceptable to those living here. There are subtle differences even between cultures that are very similar. For instance, in the UK which has similar cultural expectations, it is considered polite to thank and acknowledge a vehicle driver who stops to allow someone to cross a pedestrian crossing. In New Zealand it is not so, and generally people do not thank you for letting them cross. Culture signals the things that are acceptable and the things that are not. Looking at it in its simplest form, we might say that to be honest, polite and giving are three pillars of our expectations of each other. We can expand on each of these three and say that honesty is respect for other people, their views, property and dignity; that being polite signals that we care about how others feel; and giving acknowledges that in our world we both give and receive. In each of our families we have expectations of each other – we know how things should be. It is into these cultural settings that we are introducing our child. Our task is to train them in the ways of our family and the society in which we live.

Whatever we are is the pattern we set for our child to follow and copy. For this reason, we must be careful. If, for instance, we form a set of rigid goals or laws for our children, we are setting both them and ourselves up for a very difficult time because law stifles free expression and development and in broad terms, generates a rebellious spirit. Love and grace are essential in bringing up our child. Grace can be described as goodwill, loving-kindness and favour but law does not have that and is simply a set of rules that must be kept, breeding rigidity and failure. No, I am not advocating a rule-free childhood but simply pointing out that rigidity stifles freedom of expression. When eighteen-year-olds go off to university they go to study a subject or discipline. They know why they are there and what they have to do to pass and receive their degree. Our child has no idea that we are preparing them for life as an adult, or what the goal is. They have no exams to sit at the end. The result of good parenting in this first period of life is character; that unique combination of traits and qualities that distinguishes our child as an individual and forms their reputation, good or bad.

Chapter 7

Train a child in the way they should go

It can be argued that we get what we produce. Often this happens without us realising it, for the simple reason that we are unaware of what is going on. We auto-parent without understanding or having a goal in sight. Having our eyes opened to the realities of our own upbringing, situation and environment and the effect they will have on our children, enables us to change direction for ourselves and our children. There are, of course, no guarantees. In the end our children must make their own way in this world. However, our task is to give them the best possible start and good principles to base their decisions on.

It must be remembered that our children are not machines. They have feelings, ideas and emotions and will always seek to push the boundaries. Have you noticed how children try to get their own way, even from a very young age? A very young child will cry to get what they want and will persist in it unless it is unfruitful.

The following story is not applicable in our society and would be considered child abuse, and rightly so, but for this Native American tribe it was a matter of life and death. I tell it because it illustrates the principle that crying, necessary to communication, should never be allowed to be used by a child to manipulate or dominate the family into conforming to a child's will. As a young man I was very interested in the Apache tribe of North America. They were a warlike tribe who were under constant threat of attack from their enemies. A child's cry could give away their position to the enemy, so they had to stop their new-borns from crying. They did this by pinching their children's noses and covering their mouths as soon as they began to cry. The children soon learnt that if they cried it meant somebody was going to grab their nose and cover their mouth, and as this was not pleasant, they stopped crying. Basically, crying was unfruitful so there was no point in doing it. Such an action is unwarranted in our society, but I hope you get the point that our reactions to inappropriate crying can sometimes stimulate further unnecessary crying. If there is a real need we should react to meet that need, so that our child knows that they can rely on us when there is pain or illness, fear or insecurity. However, if the crying is because the child cannot get their own way, then how we react determines whether or not they will continue to do it again and again in the future.

A caution here – our children need to express need, such as hunger or pain, and a cry in the early months is their only means of doing this. However, there is a big difference between that which is 'need' and that which is 'want', and as a child develops we begin to realise the difference.

I am sure you have met the two-year-old who will stand and scream and scream until the parent gives the child what they want. We call it a 'temper tantrum' and I well remember a very young child, of around three years of age, trying this on. His parents' reaction was, "Okay; if you want to protest that you are not getting your own way, that's fine, but it will have no effect and bring no reward." They told him to go to the end of the garden until he could control himself and then they would talk about it. This came as a great shock to him but he quickly realised that he wasn't going to get his own way and the temper tantrum quickly stopped. Reward was gained when he controlled his temper and communicated in a fitting manner. We have to remember that we are dealing with little human beings who have all the attributes of the human race. They hurt and feel, have emotions like fear, joy, anger, love, impatience, jealousy and desire, and have a will of their own. However, it is dangerous for them to be allowed to have their own way when they have not yet learnt where that desire will lead.

A child may well be fascinated by the plug socket on the wall but they do not know that it could do them serious harm and even kill them, were they to succeed in having their own way. Who has that knowledge? The answer is the parents and the adults around them who have learnt the dangers of electricity. There are, of course, many such lessons to learn in life. Some are practical like electricity; others are more subtle, like not hurting other people's feelings and being polite rather than rude. Parents know that their goal for their children is to become well-balanced, caring adults. There is a principle in the Bible that explains to us how this happens:

'Train a child in the way he should go, and when he is old he will not turn from it'. (Proverbs 22:6)

Let's have a look at the meaning of the original Hebrew word that is translated 'train'. It is to 'hedge in, straighten him/her in'.

Remember, we are talking about an under-five-year-old child, not a teenager. This Hebrew word expresses that a young child needs guidelines that channel them in the right direction. To allow them outside the guidelines is for them to be independent, and they are clearly not equipped for that. Guidelines keep our children from harm; physically and psychologically.

The proverb gives the direction '... in the way he should go ...' We can see the way the child should go so we point them in the right direction. We put hedges in place that channel the child into the way we feel is right for them to go. The way that we set these hedges for our child needs to be in a positive, loving way that will bring contentment and safety, even if there is a little frustration for them on the way. We are the ones who set the hedges in place and we do not allow our child to stray outside of them. The difficulty is that our child cannot see the hedges because they are not visible. We cannot communicate verbally with them as they are not yet capable of understanding verbal reasoning. The hedges are in our mind; he or she can go there but not there; do that but not that. What we have to do is convince our child of it. Let me explain it through this illustration:

We had a low mantelpiece that was very reachable for a toddler, and on this mantelpiece were some breakable wooden animals. We decided we were not going to move them but were going to teach the children that they were not to be touched. When they went toward them we simply but firmly said, "No," and if they were persistent, there may have been a little tap to reinforce the point. Eventually we succeeded and they left the animals alone. In truth it was not as easy as it sounds; we still have those animals and one has its ear missing – and you can guess how that happened. What we had done was set a hedge in place. Our children could not see it, but we convinced them it was there. Such hedges bring security to a child and if we do not have such hedges it puts our child in an insecure position. We can apply the hedge principle to many areas and concepts, some of which we will discuss later in this book – this is, of course, a principle and not an exact science and we have to consistently work at it.

The proverb finishes with the end result; 'when he is old he will not depart from it'. In other words, the principle is, 'What is put into the child remains in the adult'. It starts with parents having principles which they want their children to have as well.

When our son was born we had some friends who also had a son. He was walking by six months and into everything. No discipline or punishment seemed to touch him and he seemed impossible to control. He did exactly what he wanted. He would go to the fridge and take out eggs and smash them on the floor. His parents would take him away and smack him (of course we are not allowed to do this now) but still he came back to the fridge, crying, and did exactly the same thing, again and again. He had no apparent fear and it could only be called a battle for control. At six months he prised open a cupboard door and was found trying to drink paraffin from a can. He was determined not to be stopped. His mother came around to us crying in sheer frustration, and said one thing that has stayed with me all these years – "He will not win, we will win." By being *consistent* in attitude and sticking to their principles they did indeed win! Was it easy? No, it was not, but they did not give in. They were the parents and they knew the way he should go and he was not going to go his own way no matter how hard he tried. What they did do was to continue to love, praise, encourage, understand, listen, train and correct. How did it work out? He turned out to be one of the nicest adults you could ever know – good mannered, helpful and well balanced.

Is it guaranteed? Unfortunately, the answer is no. However, it is very hard to break the pattern set for us in childhood.

When our children become adults, they have to determine their own course. Our task is to ground them in the best possible way. We then give them a chance of finding a fulfilling life. I heard one person who had a child who was rude, sulky, had continual temper tantrums and never went to sleep until the parents did, say to another person who had a child who was the opposite, "You're lucky, you have a good one; you should try mine." Were they really born differently? Are children born bad or good? I could see, in this case, that one family worked at good parenting and the other didn't even try to correct and guide their child. The way the children behaved was a direct result of the way the parents allowed them to be.

Is this how we would like to hear others describe our grown-up child? – 'He is a person who respects other people because he has an integrity within him which is the result of a deep inner honesty'.

This means that they are loyal to their principles, to their word and to their friends. Does this happen by accident?

Is it because they have a particular disposition?

Is it just because they were born that way?

Or, is it because they were trained in the way they should go?

However, it cannot be stated enough that this is not dry academic rule-based training but training done in an atmosphere of love, stability and security. This is crucial because it is in this atmosphere that human beings truly thrive and grow in both character and gifting. Our child will have no idea they are being trained for adult life but as we lovingly train them, this love will help channel them in the right direction.

Chapter 8

Brain development

How does our child learn?

In the preschool years they learn through the following:

Copying

The new member of the family does not know how to speak so he/she learns by copying those closest to them. So, is it any surprise that a child with French parents does not suddenly speak English? No, they learn French because that is the language they hear. If a child has parents of mixed race and if both languages are spoken, they will be bilingual. What about all those different accents? A child naturally picks them up too. They copy the accent of the parents. New Zealanders will not speak with an English or Australian accent unless that is what their parents speak. When the immigrant children of an English family go to a New Zealand school their accent gradually changes to a New Zealand accent, whereas, the accent of adults emigrating will generally hardly change because it is firmly established in them. When I go to the golf course and hear someone speak with a strong English, Irish or Scottish accent and I ask, "How long have you been here?" they often reply something like, "Forty years." The accent was formed in the child and is now established in the adult.

As children grow and develop, they copy many things. I sometimes find myself watching my son and thinking, *'Goodness, that's me,'* particularly if he is doing something embarrassing! So, beware; we are teaching our children subconsciously through who we are and what we do, how we do things, and our attitudes to others. We are teaching our children without realising that we are doing so, because they are copying us, and not just how we talk, how we do things or how we behave, but also our attitudes and eventually our life concepts. When I first started to preach I found I was copying the pastor of our church. I admired him and it was a natural thing to do, but eventually I began to develop my own preaching style. So it will be with our children; they simply copy what is going on around them. That is how they learn.

Influence

Influence is very similar to copying. The Collins dictionary defines the word 'influence' as, 'the effect of a person, group of people or a thing on another'. Peer pressure is an example. A group at school is doing something so we feel compelled to go along with the crowd.

As a young man just out of boarding school, I became friends with a group of Liverpool Irish Dockers' sons who were heavy drinkers. Being raised in a boarding school I had never been a drinker but after spending a lot of time with them and wanting to 'fit in', I started to drink heavily as well. Without that influence I doubt that I would ever have drank the way I did in those early years. If this influence is true for young adults, how much more for a child who knows nothing and is being influenced by everyone and everything around them.

There are also situations which influence you subconsciously. What, for instance, is being taught to the six and seven-year-old children in this incident that happened on a London street? – I was walking near a school. Coming toward me along the pavement was a party of schoolchildren aged about six or seven years. There were four teachers with them and the pavement was narrow. The children were walking in twos holding hands, and there was a teacher at the front and one at the rear. Neither the teachers nor the children took any notice of me at all and I was forced to step off the pavement and walk on the road until they had all passed. They neither thanked me nor acknowledged me in any way. I remember passing that same school some weeks later. As I approached the school gates a teacher stepped out, looked at me, stuck out her hand to stop me and called a class of children out of the gate. I was forced to watch and wait until they were all out, and then in order to overtake them, walk on the road. The adults were in charge and the children were well behaved, but what was the lesson the teachers were teaching the children without realising they were doing so? That it was acceptable to ignore adults. Today we see the results of this daily on our streets and in our shopping malls. Watch in any shopping mall and you will observe that people in general do not consider each other. The elderly are often not even noticed. It is not that we openly teach these things – we may even be horrified that this is the effect of our actions – but our children are being influenced by them. What if the teachers had noticed me and asked the children to let me through and I had been able to say, "Thank you?" That would have been teaching a different attitude altogether. Without intending to, those teachers were teaching the children how to react to others; to ignore people if they were not directly involved with them. Over time this has become the general attitude of society.

- Do we swear and curse?
- Do we talk about people in a derogatory way in front of our children?
- Do we lie?
- Do we ignore people?
- Are we violent in attitude?
- Do we smoke?
- Do we drink excessively?

Think about what we are potentially passing on to our children. It brings into sharp focus what is unacceptable, and brings to mind the things that are desirable, such as honesty, integrity, kindness, patience, joyfulness, peacefulness, faithfulness, gentleness and self-control.

Be aware of the things we do that could influence our children, and what we feel is acceptable behaviour and what is not. Being aware helps us to demonstrate in our own lives what we want to pass on to our children.

Environment

By environment we mean the external conditions in which we live. We cannot always change those situations very easily. However, the fact that we are aware of the possible influence of our environment enables us to take whatever actions we can to combat the negative environment and encourage the positive.

It is an uncomfortable truth that environment creates a generational pull. If we were brought up in a gang-oriented society then the chances are that our children will likely go in that same direction; not always, but it is the general trend. If our environment is academic, with parents who are well educated and in professional vocations, then that is the general direction in which our children will go. Of course, the environment is often dictated by money. Poverty does not always allow a family to move away from its environment. Often, we are not aware of how our environment is playing such a crucial role in our children's destiny. To them their environment is normal. The question is; can we bring children up in a difficult environment but then change the direction for future generations? The answer has to be 'yes'.

For twenty years I led a church in inner London. It was an environment of high-rise blocks of flats and in those days, the council owned 95% of the properties. There were no estate agents in the district because there were no houses to sell. Some of those blocks of flats were in a dreadful state and when I first visited some of them, I was appalled at the poverty and degradation in which these families lived, and yet there I found families who did buck the generational trend. Admittedly, these were mainly Christian families who worked hard to instil in their children standards of behaviour that would see them eventually overcome their environment. But it was not only Christian families. I met others who also saw the need for a change of situation for their children and worked hard to enable that to happen. However, there were many families who had no idea that their environment was having such a detrimental effect on their children. That was the environment they grew up in and so they assumed their children would grow up there just like them. They did not see that it was potentially a trap which in fact could be broken.

It takes dedication and a lot of stubbornness not to give in to the environment around you. My Liverpool Irish mate died recently. He drank throughout his whole life – it was the environment he grew up in. It had gripped him all his life and eventually contributed to his death. His father and his grandfather had both been affected by this environment. My friend was born into it and it stayed with him. I was, for a while, caught up in this drinking culture, but fortunately for me I became a Christian and was influenced by a completely different culture, for which I am very grateful. I well remember a young man who became a Christian from a family that were heavy drinkers who lived from hand-to-mouth. He began to go in a completely different direction and became very successful in business. Some years later I heard of the family again; he was doing well but the rest of his siblings had remained influenced by the family's drinking culture.

What has all that got to do with our under-five year old? Just this – recognise the influences of environment.

Teaching

Teaching helps somebody to learn and demonstrates how to do something. So it is with our parenting – we are showing our children how things are done; how to hold a spoon, tie shoelaces, as well as many other things but as well as practical skills there are concepts. For instance, if we borrow something from somebody and we break it, we will teach our children one of two basic things; that it matters or that it doesn't. If we borrow a DVD and lose or damage it and our attitude is 'we must replace it', then we are teaching that it matters, and that it is important to respect other people's property. If, on the other hand, our attitude is 'tough!', then we are teaching that it does not matter and our child will grow up thinking the same. We lent a heater to a family and something burnt out on it. They replaced it even when we said that it was not necessary. There is a strong possibility that the children of that family will have the same attitude as the parents. Never guaranteed, because I know a family who are very generous but have one child who is clearly not at all generous, and yet, if we do not demonstrate such qualities, there will be no example for our children.

As a teenager, my son was often late for school, but his teacher used to sign him in even if he was not there. The lesson that teacher was teaching my son was that it was okay to be late.

It would also be wise to consider what is being taught while our children watch TV, DVDs, listen to music or watch music videos?

Do we always know what our children are being taught by the things they watch or listen to? They can be good or bad influences.

Spirituality

Some say that with spiritual things you can wait until your children are old enough to understand, but we are surrounded by the work of the Creator – how can we ignore that and never speak of Him? His Word, the Bible, is full of precepts on how we are to live, how we are to treat each other and, above all, how we can relate to God through our Lord Jesus Christ. Thus, praying for (and with) our children and reading His Word is vital for their understanding of the Creator. It is also important to tell our own story of how we became one of His children and also some of the things we have seen God do in others. Our children will pick up more than we think, so do not wait; do it from the start.

The people of the Bible had principles they wanted to pass on from generation to generation. Some of these principles had to do with their relationship to God, their respect for Him, the way they honoured Him in their day-to-day lives and the importance of nothing coming between God and His people. These principles are found in what we know as the Ten Commandments. The first three revolve around the fact that there is only one God, and therefore no one should make a god of anything else in their life. Respecting the name of God is also important in maintaining respect towards God.

The fourth commandment encourages everyone to have a day off and keep it separate from the routines of every other day – the idea being that they could have time for God, one another and family on that day.

The other six commandments are about relationships between people and the maintaining of standards of behaviour in society in order to create a safe, ordered world for everyone to live in.

The fifth commandment is about showing respect to parents and includes the older members of society as well. The sixth forbids the taking of another person's life, indicating that life is precious and important, and the seventh teaches the importance of respecting relationships, and in particular marriage.

The eighth commandment is about not stealing and respecting other people's property. It was also important to the people of the Bible to maintain good relationships with neighbours and the wider community in which they lived. The ninth involves not telling lies about each other in court or lying for their own advantage, and the tenth is to do with rejecting what we today would call 'keeping up with the Joneses' – being jealous and wanting someone else's possessions.

These are all principles or laws that were designed to create a society in which people could feel safe and secure. We can see that if they had kept these laws it would have been a great place to live. It would be like going back to the days when nobody locked their doors because they trusted the people living around them. Did it just happen? Was it automatic that the next generation would follow on? No, so the Bible tells us how they went about passing these things on to their children and it is very appropriate for us today.

The Bible says, '... these principles ... are to be on your hearts. Impress them on your children. Talk about them when you sit at home and when you walk along the road, when you lie down and when you get up'. (Deuteronomy 6:6-7)

The people of the Bible were encouraged to pass these principles on to their children. How did they do this? By talking to their children about these principles as opportunities arose in their day-to-day lives.

We must note though, that it is difficult to pass on what is not in our own heart. It has to be in us to start with. What we are trying to pass on should not be an idea outside of ourselves but something we understand and practice.

- Are we rude and ignore people?
- Do we speak in a disrespectful manner about other people?
- Do we lie to get out of trouble?
- Do we cheat to get our own way?

It is what is in our own heart that we will pass on to the next generation. We need to talk to our children about what is important to us using everyday happenings in a gentle and loving manner.

Let me give you an illustration of this. I know a family where the mum was brought up with the view that drinking alcohol was wrong. At one time they lived opposite a pub and she would often comment about the people coming out a little worse for wear, and while she was saying this she would shudder and make a face. (The reason for this was that, as a child, her mother suffered terribly at the hands of drunken guardians, and her mother had passed her rightful distaste onto her child.) Often this would happen when their young son was within hearing. The day came when he started to express the same feelings about alcohol and condemn anyone who had a drink or went into a pub. When he walked by a pub and he smelt alcohol he would make a face and make some negative comment, and even shudder just like his mother. Her dislike was justified as far as her mother was concerned but she had passed this onto her son. The father had to sit down and make a few corrections so that the son did not condemn everyone who had an alcoholic drink.

Children 'pick up' things naturally. The way we talk and the attitudes we express in word, deed and disposition will all be taken in. It is often said of our children that they are too young to understand. However, the reality is that they are taking it all in and learning how to conduct themselves in this world and, whether we like it or not, we are teaching them how to do it. How we as parents relate to one another is the standard they are assimilating for the future. Do we give off negative or positive vibes? Think of the times we talk in front of our children. They are picking up every negative or positive attitude we have, both toward them and others. They may not be able to tell us what they are learning, but I assure you, it is all going in. If we speak spitefully about others, eventually we will hear our children do the same.

Children learn attitudes and concepts from birth and it is a process which is built on little by little. The values, concepts and attitudes we as parents have are the values, concepts and attitudes our children will learn and be trained in. The platform is being built and character is being formed. It is these first five years of their lives when we are in control of the influences that enter the fertile new brain of our children. Later this may change when our children are surrounded by conflicting influences like peer pressure from school, not to mention television and the Internet, and of course these influences only increase as time goes by.

We need to make the most of these first five years to lay the platform for the character we want to see in our children. We should not try to change the disposition of our children but endeavour to input into that disposition honesty, integrity, trustworthiness and loyalty – the marks of good character.

Chapter 9

Character Building

The years from birth to starting school are vital in the development of our child's character. There are five facets of character that are very desirable in a person no matter what their general disposition. They are respect, honesty, integrity, trustworthiness and loyalty. If these are important in adult life, then we as parents need to know how to teach our children them. The question arises as to how we, as parents, can pass on to our children the principles which will be their guide in life and help form their character. We will look at each facet in turn to understand what each one means, as this will help us to demonstrate them to our children.

It is important to understand the basic principle; what we are is what we will pass on to our children. If we are respectful, honest, of high integrity, trustworthy and loyal then our children will generally be inclined to follow our example, as we reinforce these principles day by day. If, however, the reverse is true and we are not honest, do not respect other people and are not trustworthy or loyal, then that is what we will pass on.

Respect

One aspect of respect is a deep admiration for somebody whom you admire, somebody who has earned respect by some achievement or has other manifestly outstanding attributes. The Collins dictionary also tells us that it means 'due regard for the feelings and rights of others, to avoid harming and interfering with another person'. The first part is not something that can be demanded of a person; it is earned and recognised. However, the second part of respect is our general day-to-day reaction to the people around us.

On a visit to the USA many years ago we went to stay with a family that we did not know. They were relatives of my cousin's husband. There were three children in the family, aged from about six to twelve years of age, and they were a delight. At the door they greeted us with their parents, conversed with us and made us feel very welcome. Within a very short space of time we were having musical recitals and had a wonderful family meal with all the children taking part. There was no awkwardness or sulkiness. They were polite and, yes, respectful of us as visitors. Did that just happen? Of course not! Firstly, that was who the parents were, and secondly, I can guarantee that the parents had trained them to be respectful of other people.

We teach respect for others by the way we ourselves respect others, but we can also actively follow that up by instructing our children how to do so. I remember visiting my prayer partner one morning at 7am. His daughter was sitting watching TV. I said, "Hello." There was no reply, which did not concern me too much, but in an instant her mother was there. "Say hello to Bob, it is rude to ignore people." I had to stand there for at least ten minutes before I got a much begrudged, "Hello, Bob." However, the next week I arrived and there was the girl watching TV, so, with much apprehension, I said, "Good morning." Back came an instant reply, "Good morning, Bob." That child is now in her teens and I am willing to guarantee that she does not ignore people, but is polite and respectful. I can just imagine the American family we visited going through the same thing with their children during those early years.

I have seen it in my children's upbringing of our five granddaughters, who now range from sixteen years to twenty-five years of age. All five are respectful of those around them and are a delight to be with. It was not always easy for their parents, and they had to fight the battle of wills just as my prayer partner and his wife had to, but it was worth it. Contrast that with some families where, when you visit their homes, the children do not even acknowledge you and it is as though you do not exist. I have visited families where a child does not even look at you, let alone speak, and it is not just shyness in that one child but often all the children have the same attitude towards outsiders. When I have seen this in young children the parents often say the children are just shy. This may well be the case, but other people will not accept this as an excuse for the children not acknowledging other people.

Remember that this is not a matter of being shaped into a single mould. Some people are shy while others are bold; some introverts, others extroverts. Naturally, an extrovert finds it easier to interact with others than an introvert. I am an introvert by nature and would hate somebody to force me into the mould of an extrovert. However, we can all be polite and acknowledge those around us and that is where it starts for our children – as simply as in the case of my prayer partner's wife, who insisted that her child say, 'Hello' to somebody visiting their home. That was all that was required to get the point across at that stage. Her children do not have to stand and say, "Good morning Bob, you are very welcome to our house and I hope you have a good visit." No, all she had to say was, 'Hello'. Take the school children walking down the street faced with an adult coming in the opposite direction – "Children, make room for the gentleman to get through please," was all that was necessary to teach the point that we should not ignore other people, but be polite and respectful of others. From there it progresses to our child taking part in meals and not allowing them to hide away in their rooms when visitors call.

Of course, we have to recognise that it can be boring for our child to have to sit with adults all afternoon just because they are visitors, so after the child has acknowledged everyone and been polite for a while they can be given permission to go off and play if they want to. Recently, we took our youngest granddaughter out with her other grandmother. She had her iPod Touch with her but had been taught that it was rude to read or play with her iPod Touch while in company. However, it was obvious that it was hard sitting there with three elderly relatives nattering away, so I said, "Go on, play with your iPod." She got the point, but there was no reason to make it painful for her.

It is as simple as insisting on a 'please' and a 'thank you' in everyday life.

"Would you like a lolly?"

"Yes!"

"Oh, you've left your manners behind; sorry you cannot have lollies without your manners."

Of course, manners are soon found and the result is that our child gets their lolly. However, the principle remains; no manners, no lolly. The lesson is fun but the principle is there. Our children will not understand the concepts behind it all; we are simply training them in the way they should go in life, putting hedges in place, and pointing them in the right direction. We may have to fight battles sometimes but the reward will be when we see that it has become the norm for our children to show respect to others around them.

Chapter 10

Honesty

Honesty is the quality of truthfulness. It could also be said that it is the qualities of being open and straightforward. There is nothing hidden in an honest person, no dark places they would hate to be exposed.

Its opposite is dishonesty. We all tend to want to cover our mistakes by diverting attention away from ourselves, and to do this we lie. It seems to be instinctive in human beings and has to do with fear and the reluctance of being caught out. We fear the concept of 'let the punishment fit the crime' and we do not readily believe that 'honesty is the best policy'.

Yet now, after all these years, for me it is manifestly obvious that honesty is the 'best policy' in life. Dishonesty makes for a complicated life – we have to remember our lies and then run with them, and that is hard work. Dishonesty also results in those around us not trusting us, because even when we get away with lying, others often know we have lied but cannot prove it. We need to convince our children that honesty is important until it becomes a part of their character. Of course, the big question is; how do we do that?

Let's begin with the fear of being caught out because of the possible consequences and the possible punishment for what we have done. If a person fears the punishment or consequences of an incident this can result in lying. Our task with our children is to reverse that fear and to make the consequence of lying worse than the punishment of owning up to something.

In boarding school one of the lessons I learnt was that if I was honest about something I had done wrong, I usually got away with it, or, if I did not completely get away with it, the consequences were much lighter than if I was caught lying. So, I practised honesty because it resulted in a better outcome. I did not practice honesty because I was good or virtuous but simply because the punishment for lying or getting caught doing wrong was much worse than when I was being honest.

To try to convince somebody that it is better to be honest can be like speaking to a brick wall. However, if our experience is that honesty is better than being untruthful, (as happened to me at boarding school), then the lesson sticks and truthfulness becomes a way of life. It was only later that I began to notice that people began to see me as someone that could be trusted, and I came to appreciate what a great thing that was.

This, then, is the clue to convincing our children that honesty is better than lying. We create an environment where honesty is rewarded and dishonesty is something to be avoided as it incurs a greater punishment.

The way we did this with our own children was that, as far as we were able, they never got away with lying. To be dishonest did not pay, but being honest did pay in that they often got away without punishment or there was just a mild telling off. We did have some battles to fight. One day I found that somebody had picked at the wallpaper while sitting on the toilet. Now I was sure it wasn't Mary and it certainly wasn't me, so it must have been one of the children. I called them both together. "Who picked the wallpaper off the wall while sitting on the toilet?" I asked. "Not me!" "Nor me!" They replied. "Well, one of you did and we are not moving until I find out who did it," I responded. There followed quite a battle until eventually one of them confessed to the deed. One of course needed to be apologised to, having had to sit through the 'inquisition'. For the other 'the punishment fitted the crime', and this was not so much about the wallpaper but the lie. If the guilty one had owned up it would have been a mild lecture on the difficulty of having to repaper the whole wall and 'please do not do it again'. We tried to be consistent. If they were caught out lying they never got away with it and they were punished more severely than if they had told the truth. As far as I am aware, my children have grown up to be honest adults.

Were they aware that this was our plan, that this was one of the invisible hedges we put in place? No, I am sure they weren't, but honesty gradually became part of their character. We can make 'honesty the best policy' by simply making sure dishonesty is always punished and that honesty is always commended. In that way our children learn to be honest in day-to-day life, and this will usually result in our children becoming honest people.

Chapter 11

Integrity

Integrity is very similar to honesty – The Collins dictionary defines it as 'adherence to moral principles' whereas honesty is defined as 'the quality of being unimpaired, soundness'. Integrity goes beyond simply not telling lies; it is living according to good principles.

When we were first married, Mary was ill and I borrowed a record from a friend to cheer her up. As I was putting it on the turntable I accidentally scratched it. It is at these times our moral principles are revealed – the integrity that governs our lives. There was, for us, no question – the record had to be replaced, even though it was going to be really hard to find the money. We had damaged somebody else's property and it needed to be put right. Another example was when everyone at work went freelance and we were responsible for paying our own tax. My work colleague lied about the amount of work he did and as a result paid very little tax. My well-established principle in life was to be honest and so I ended up paying three times as much as he did. Some would say, 'more fool you', but my integrity had to be maintained. Integrity takes us beyond the point of not lying and leads us to living a life that is sound in everything we do and is not thrown off course by inconvenience, difficulty or calamity.

In some UK seaside resorts such as Brighton they sell a sweet confectionery called rock, which is anything up to half a metre long. The distinctive thing about rock is that somehow the name of the resort goes right through the middle of the stick. No matter where you break it, it still says 'Brighton'. It is not just on the surface but goes right through the stick. Integrity is like that. It is having honesty that permeates a person's life. It is in how you relate to others, how you react to crisis, and even how you are when nobody can see you or when those in authority, like parents, are not around.

What has this got to do with children under five? They need to learn about integrity right from the start. How are they going to learn such principles? They will learn through demonstration and example. How we conduct our day-to-day lives demonstrates our integrity to our children and this will, in turn, rub off on them. We teach it in our everyday life, starting with very simple lessons such as; if you borrow something then you should return it; otherwise you are stealing or, if you break something that belongs to someone else then it needs to be replaced. As we live out our lives like this in front of our children, we are building these principles in our children's lives little by little. Communication is also important – by explaining the 'what' and 'why' of different situations, we teach them not to live in such a way that hurts or offends other people unnecessarily.

The conversation might go like this:

"Oh dear, I have broken that jug I borrowed from Auntie Jean, I will have to go and buy her a new one."

"Why? Hasn't she got any other jugs?"

"Because when we break something we have borrowed, it is very important we replace it. Otherwise, Auntie Jean will have to spend some of her money to replace it and that would not be right, would it? How would you feel if John broke your toy and gave it back broken?"

"I would be very upset with him."

"Well, that is why it is very important to do what the Bible says – that we should do to others as we would want them to do to us."

It is conversations like this that teach integrity to our children. We can also demonstrate integrity if our child breaks someone else's possessions by making them part of the restoration process; by having them help us buy a replacement and then personally giving that replacement back to the owner.

Our integrity extends to the way we treat people and the principles that govern how we talk to, and about, other people. Are our comments hurtful, spiteful, undermining or hateful, or are they kind, helpful, supportive and caring? Whatever they are is what we are teaching our children in our day-to-day lives. Our integrity and thought patterns are being absorbed by them

Integrity is an extension of honesty that goes right through a person's life and is essential to the building of character.

Remember that character is the combination of traits and qualities distinguishing the individual nature of a person – reputation, especially a good one. We pass on our 'good' integrity until it becomes the norm in our children's lives. Practical day-to-day demonstrations with simple corrections make the point and by the time our child starts school, his or her general character attributes will be becoming well formed.

Trustworthiness and Loyalty

Two other attributes of character which mark a person's life stem from honesty and integrity. The first of these is trustworthiness, which means being able to be relied upon as honest, truthful and reliable. This accolade comes from other people about a person. You know the kind of thing – two people are talking; one mentions somebody to another and they say, "Yes you can rely on him; he won't let you down." This is a direct result of a person's honesty and integrity, something that is deep within them and, like that stick of rock, it goes right through them. This is the reputation that comes with character, and for me, was one of the benefits that honesty bestowed on me. I discovered that people trusted me and that was, and is, something I value very much.

The second attribute is loyalty, which means a strong feeling of support or allegiance or a feeling of support toward others within a framework of truth. There is a negative to this and that is the kind of loyalty that is blind. You know the sort of thing – 'I am going to tell you a secret that must be shared with nobody else', or, 'If you join us you must never tell anyone what we do or say'. If loyalty overrides honesty we get into the area of loyalty covering up wrong and then honesty vanishes and dishonesty replaces it. The correct concept is to instil into our children a right sense of loyalty that is based on honesty and openness. Loyalty to the truth is vital if they are to have an integrity that stands the pressure of school and adult life, and this lesson begins as soon as their interaction starts with other children. Our child comes crying hysterically and says, "Tommy hit me!" In defence of our own child, we could rush over to Tommy and give him a severe telling off that causes him, in turn, to cry. What does this teach our child? It teaches them that we will support them and protect them, and of course that is very important, but it also teaches them that they can get another child into trouble just by simply bursting into tears and running to us. What if we were to approach it in a different manner? Our first action would be to calm our child down and find out what happened. We might ask them, "Did you do something to upset Tommy?" and "How is Tommy feeling now – should we go and find out how he is?" We would then get them together and seek to reconcile them and find out the truth. Thus, we are teaching our children to care for others as well as themselves and getting them involved with the resolution. We are teaching loyalty to our children because we want them to grow up seeing both sides of the story as well as helping them to understand how others are feeling. If Tommy is a bully, we are teaching our children how to stand up to bullies by getting them to talk to us about what has happened. We are also teaching that loyalty should not be blind, that the truth needs to be out in the open, and only then can healing come to all.

Chapter 12

Consistency

Before we consider this very important word, we need to fully understand that for the first five years of our child's life, we as parents are the ones who are responsible for our children's development; pointing and training them into the direction they need to go, not for our benefit but for theirs. The question arises as to what is best for them and what will benefit them in life? At the moment they know nothing of life and its pitfalls. It is sometimes good to look at the negative side of things as it helps to define the positive.

The Houston Police department produced a pamphlet entitled *Twelve rules for raising delinquent children.* It states:

1. Begin at infancy to give your child everything he wants. In this way, he will grow up to believe the world owes him a living.
2. When he picks up bad language laugh at him. This will make him feel he is clever.
3. Avoid using the word 'wrong'. It may cause a guilt complex. This will condition him to believe later, when he is arrested for stealing a car, that society is against him and he is being persecuted.
4. Pick up everything he leaves lying around; books, clothes and shoes. Do everything for him so that he will be experienced in throwing all responsibility on others.
5. Let him read any printed matter he can get his hands on. Be careful that the cutlery and glasses are sterilised, but let his mind feast on rubbish.
6. Quarrel frequently in the presence of your child. In this way he will not be shocked when the home is broken up later.
7. Give your child all the spending money he wants. Never let him earn his own. Why should he have things as tough as you had them?

8. Satisfy his every craving for food, drink and comfort. See that every sensual desire is gratified. Denial may lead to harmful frustration.
9. Never give him any spiritual training. Wait until he is twenty-one and then let him decide for himself.
10. Take his part against neighbours, teachers and police. They are prejudiced against your child.
11. When he gets into real trouble, apologise for yourself saying, "I never could do anything with him."
12. Prepare for a life of grief. You will be likely to have it. (1)

Without them being aware of it, our children rely on us for guidance, protection, sustenance, safety and direction. Which direction are we channelling our children into? The proverb we looked at states, 'Train up a child in the way he should go; even when he is old he will not depart from it'. Do we kid ourselves that it is easy? No, it is not easy and the reason is because our children are not automatons that can be pushed at will in a certain direction. They need to be channelled, persuaded, encouraged and coaxed into the best direction for them. We should remember that it is harder later on to change something already ingrained in our child's character. It is easier to understand what we are seeking to achieve from the start and work at that, rather than needing to change it later.

For this reason, the key word which we should understand is 'consistency'. We should write it so large that it becomes the only word on the page; it is that important. Imagine for a moment that you have a new computer. Its memory is empty and you have to form an ordered filing system with the goal of being able to find the file you want and when you want it. The one thing that must be avoided is confusion. When I suggested to Mary that maybe we only needed one computer, her reply was, "the mess your filing system is in, no thank you, I would never be able to find anything!" Inconsistencies just will not do and that is only for a computer that does not have feelings or a will of its own, even though Mary often thinks it does!

Think about your new baby. Inside that beautiful head is a brand-new brain that has started to take in everything around it. It is slow at first but soon starts to gather speed until it is taking in more and more. It is like a sponge as it continues to soak up everything, little by little, and the reality is that it

Never stops. It is forming language, facts, concepts and memories. It also remembers hurts and fears.

Hearing, sight, touch and smells all contribute to the way our children's brains form. At this age our children have no ability to figure out concepts and distinguish what is right and what is wrong for them. When our children receive mixed messages, with no ability to distinguish what is good or bad, the result is confusion. Unlike a computer our children have dispositions and wills of their own and a capacity for wanting their own way almost from birth. Now imagine what inconsistent messages will do. One minute something is okay but then the next, it's not. We need to know what is best for our children and be consistent in its application. Otherwise, we confuse and discourage them and their confidence is undermined.

I have said that there are five facets of character that are very desirable in a person, no matter what their general disposition or skill – respect, honesty, integrity, trustworthiness and loyalty. To achieve these, we will need a consistent approach, as confusion will only muddy the waters. Our children are people who have feelings and personalities which may differ from our own. Yet the question for now is, what will their character be? What will their reputation be with those around them? To achieve good character there needs to be consistent input in the early years.

Let's look again at my friend's little girl who did not say, 'Hello' to me. Imagine if her parents had been inconsistent with her; one day she was required to say 'Hello' but then the next she wasn't. She would have been getting mixed, confused messages. This could have resulted in her becoming deceitful in that she might only say, 'Hello' when it suited her, and true politeness would have been lost. I sometimes come across children who will not say anything and as a result become introverted and have difficulty relating with others. It amazes me how all of our five granddaughters could hold conversations with adults and were generally polite to everyone around them from a very early age. I believe it was the result of their parents' input.

Children are secure when they are getting consistent messages, and this starts from day one. If we burn the word 'consistency' into our minds it will pay great dividends, both to us as parents and to our children. In our world today, governments often set out to solve the problem of troubled teenagers by putting programmes in place. But as one young car 'hoon' said, "We won't change, no matter what they do."

If we want to change our society, we need to start working with our under-fives to input the character traits of respect, honesty, integrity, trustworthiness and loyalty.

If we are to be consistent, then we as parents need to agree on what we will be consistent about. In any marriage there are different personalities and different ways of going about things. For instance, one parent wants to get their child into a good bedtime routine by setting a consistent pattern around bedtime. The other parent undermines this by saying, "But she's so young, I am so enjoying a cuddle – can't we just let her stay up for a while?" or one parent cannot abide their child crying and does everything to avoid it, but this causes conflict between the parents, which, of course, confuses the child.

It is virtually impossible to maintain consistency without agreement and so it is crucial that both parents agree on what behaviour they will allow, and what they will not allow in their children. Otherwise, the child will soon realise that they can play one parent off against the other. For example, the child says to one parent:

> "Can I have some lollies, please?"
>
> "No, because it's nearly dinner time."
>
> "Please, I will still eat my dinner!"
>
> "No, and that's final."

So, the child goes off with the same request to the other parent, who has proved to be a soft touch on past occasions, and is given permission to have the lollies. If we are to find consistency we will need to solve these problems. With regard to playing one parent off against the other, we need to develop the automatic question, "What did your father/mother say?" In this way our children learn that they will not get away with such tactics. It is always a serious thing for children to succeed in playing one parent off against the other, and if discovered, there should be consequences. Solving problems is not always easy, as there are often fundamental differences in each parent's approach brought about by their own experience as a child. However, it is essential to come to some agreement in our approach to parenting if consistency is to be maintained.

This principle can be applied to many areas of parenting – consistency is the secret to success.

If we understand the reasons for consistency and understand that inconsistency can cause confusion, we can overcome our differences and agree to be consistent – but without agreement it is virtually impossible.

Chapter 13

Discipline

There is a proverb that tells us, 'Wise discipline imparts wisdom; spoiled adolescents embarrass their parents'. (Proverbs 29:15)

This is not an exact translation of the original which says, 'Spare the rod and spoil the child'. The rod today is not allowed by law but the spirit of the verse is as the version quoted above, which is from The Message Bible.[5]

The word discipline means 'disciplinary correction'; in other words, bringing correction when something is wrong, or correcting when somebody is going the wrong way or doing the wrong thing. In Chapter 7 we outlined the task before us as being; 'to train our child in preparation for adulthood', and we do this by putting restrictions in place – 'You can go there, but not there; you can do that but not that'. Children need these guidelines that channel them in the right direction, and to allow children outside the guidelines is for them to behave independently when they are clearly not yet equipped to do so. Guidelines keep our children from that which harms them physically, psychologically and which harms their personalities. The proverb also gives the direction '... in the way he should go ...' We can see the way our children should go, so we point them in the right direction and correct them when they move away from the way we are setting for them. This is what discipline is about; it is not about punishment.

There is no doubt at all that our children will want to disobey us and just do what they want to do. When one of our granddaughters was a young child, she was told not to run ahead of the family nor step onto the road when they were out for a walk. However, she immediately did exactly what

5 The Message: Eugene H. Peterson. NavPress

she had been told not to do. Discipline in this context, then, was not so much about punishment but much more about guarding from danger. It was also about training our granddaughter to be safe around traffic.

However, there does come a point where guidance needs to be enforced. How do you correct such behaviour and how do we stop it happening again?

There are two words which epitomise this task and they are 'yes' and 'no'. 'Yes' is the easy one as it means 'go', it's permissible', 'it's alright'. There is usually no conflict with 'yes'. Our three-year-old wants to run free when they usually have to stay with us, but we are in a park and it is safe, so we say, "Yes, go." The problem comes when it is time to leave and he/she wants to stay and play some more and we say, "no." It is like my granddaughter, who decided she would run away from her mum when she was told, "Come here, it's time to go home." 'No' is a block which says you cannot do that or go there and, of course there will come a time when that block will be challenged. The problem for parents is how to make 'no', mean 'no'. It is important when we say, 'no' that our child does not interpret it as meaning, 'yes'. This is exactly what happened to a woman I observed waiting in a queue in a post office many years ago. Alongside the queue was a counter with all sorts of cheap toys and the woman's son, who was about four or five, found a toy he liked and took it over to his mother. The conversation went like this:

> "Can I have this?"
>
> "No."
>
> "Can I have this?"
>
> "No!"
>
> This was repeated quite a few times, then mum changed tack and it continued on like this:
>
> "Can I have this?"
>
> "How much is it?"
>
> "One pound."
>
> "Have you got a pound?"

"No."

"Well you can't have it then."

"Mum, can I have this?"

"No!"

"Mum, can I have this?"

"No!"

"Mum, can I have this?"

"Oh alright, here's a pound."

The mother had clearly demonstrated to her son previously that 'no' meant 'yes' if he was persistent enough. Would he have bothered if, in the past, his mother had said, 'no' and not changed her mind under a persistent bombardment? I would suggest that he would not have bothered after the first or second attempt.

However, if our 'no' is to remain 'no', we need to be careful in not using it too quickly. First, consider if it is going to be 'yes' or 'no', or even a 'maybe'. If it is 'no' then it must not be changed to make it mean 'yes'. Likewise, a 'yes' must not be changed to a 'no'.

During my childhood while at boarding school my parents would often say, "Yes, you are coming home for the holidays," and then change their minds and I had to stay at school. This had such a negative effect on me that years later, after marrying and having my own children, I would become miserable and unhappy whenever we went away on holiday as a family. I eventually realised that I had been subconsciously dreading something happening to stop us going on holiday. However, once I was there I was fine and able to enjoy myself. 'Yes' and 'no' may be small words but they can have a big impact. The question arises as to how we make our 'no' mean 'no' when our child is crying or lying on the ground screaming and trying to get us to give in and let them have their own way.

I said earlier that 'no' means 'stop'. One of the most common methods of insisting on that stop when our child defies us is to set in motion a timeout period which in effect forces them to stop everything for a period. The first step is to say, 'no' meaning 'stop'. It may be that our child is heading for the electric socket on the wall and we say firmly, "No, you are not to touch it because it can hurt you." We get hold of our child and take them away from the socket. Now if our child is a typical young child, guess what? They will go straight back and try to play with the socket again because they have no idea how or if it can hurt them. They need to be convinced that there is a consequence if they touch the socket, and we do not want that consequence to be an electric shock. We give them a warning; "If you touch that again, you will go and sit on the naughty stool." The naughty stool can be the bottom of the stairs, on a mat or on a chair – somewhere where they can see everything going on around them but cannot take part in it. There are no toys, drawing or other things for them to do while they are there. It is very important that the warning is given because there must always be the opportunity for them to respond. So, if they defy us yet again, as they probably will, we say, "I did warn you that if you did that again you would go to the naughty stool. So now you will have to go there for three minutes because you disobeyed me." It is suggested that the timeout period is one minute for every year of a child's age, e.g. three minutes for three-year olds and four minutes for four-year olds. If they will not stay and keep running away we must bring them back, and if necessary, hold them there without conversation or play until they are convinced that we mean it; also timing the timeout from when they sit there without us holding them. It is important that we make sure we note the time. It is no good suddenly realising that we have forgotten the time and our child has been there for ten minutes. What happens next is crucial for the timeout to work effectively. We return to our child and explain that they have had to sit there because they disobeyed us. To not do this will bring possible confusion. We need to ask them if they understand that they must do as we say; rather than explaining the danger of electricity as they will not understand unless they actually receive a shock. We then finish the timeout by asking our child to say sorry, followed by a big hug. It is then all over and not to be mentioned anymore. If it happens again we will need to go through the same procedure and keep doing it until the lesson is learned. It needs to be done without any shouting, anger or sudden reaction. We also need to be gentle but firm and not allow our child to turn it into a game. Friends of ours had a large DVD collection and their little boy delighted in pulling the DVDs out of the shelves. I advised them to follow the timeout method, which they did, and the lad eventually left those DVDs alone.

If we practice this, making it the norm from the moment our children begin to move about, we will not get to the stage where it becomes a battle of wills. This is, of course, just one method of enforcing your 'no' and is a method I would encourage as I have seen it work very well. Not enforcing our 'no' results in our children not knowing where they stand and that sociologically leaves them in a position of insecurity. If you feel this method is not for you, find a way to make your 'no' mean 'no'. There must be consequences or the lesson will not be learnt.

(For an outline of timeout see Appendix 1)

Chapter 14

The law of consequences

To every action there is a consequence. This never stops and if we do not learn and experience this law we will continually get into trouble. The 'law of consequences' is the ability to assess the result of the actions we take.

Let me illustrate this – after I had left the drinking culture of my youth I had an urge to return to it, but an older friend said to me, "Have a look at those who have already gone down that road and ask yourself; do I want to end up where they are?" So I did. I observed the older men who spent every night drinking in the pub and decided that I didn't want to end up like them. This single piece of advice expressed the 'law of consequences' in a way which enabled me to make choices based on what the probable result would be.

A consequence, according to the Collins dictionary is 'a result or effect, an unpleasant result, an inference reached by reasoning'.

This law is important because it is something we use throughout our lives. It helps us to automatically determine or assess what is likely to happen when we make decisions. However, if we do not learn it during childhood it is something we will possibly struggle with all our lives. The safe environment of childhood is a very important training ground for learning consequences. For instance, the timeout concept teaches children that there is a consequence to disobedience – that if they disobey then they are put into timeout. Eventually a child recognises what is happening and obeys because they dislike the consequences of disobeying. They may not think or express this but the habit of assessing consequences is being formed. Of course, every time they get away with disobedience they learn that a consequence does not always follow, and therefore they can take a chance. As with the young boy in the post office, a child can learn that 'no' does not actually mean 'no' and therefore the law is negated or, is at best, confused. A consistent environment means that our children learn without the danger that could come in later life if wrong decisions are made. Because honesty was highly valued in our family, every time our children were caught lying, there was a serious consequence, but if they were honest, and owned up to what they had done, they got away with it or the punishment was fairly mild. Thus, they learnt to be truthful, and chose truth over lies.

There is another parenting method that fails to teach this 'law of consequences' and it is called distraction. The idea is that if our children are heading for the electric plug, we do not say, 'no', but distract them by bringing something else to their attention. Unfortunately, this can become a game and it means that we always have to be available to distract our children from what we don't want them to do. In this method we avoid using the word 'no' because it is negative and we try to keep everything positive. The positive is 'yes', so rather than say, 'no' we point out something that we can say, 'yes' to. While I understand the importance of being positive, this method does not teach the 'law of consequences'. I knew a family who practised distraction parenting and the results were not good. As the children grew up they had no idea what was right or wrong and if they came to our house we never knew what was going to be moved or broken. They had just not learnt the 'law of consequences' and grew up to be rather insecure young people.

How do children learn the 'law of consequences'? You may well think that this cannot possibly apply to children under five, but it does, and it is very important to understand that this period of their lives is where we lay the foundations.

Timeout and training in honesty helps teach our children that there are consequences to their actions and there are many other ways it can be taught in everyday life. The sixteen-month-old has just started walking. He holds mum's hand but wants to let go. He soon learns that the consequence of this is that he falls over. Fortunately he has a nappy on which cushions the fall. The two-year-old sees a low wall while we are walking along the road. He wants to walk along it, so we put him on the wall and say, "You will hurt yourself if you fall." We are warning him of the consequences, but of course he does not yet understand what we mean so he insists on letting go of our hand and falls. Fortunately for him we are there waiting to catch him, but he is learning the 'law of consequences'. We should allow our children to be adventurous and we should not protect them from everything that may have a possible harmful outcome. However, what we do is create a safe environment for them to learn the application of the 'law of consequences'. Bring consequences into everyday conversations – we say to them, "Look what happened because he did that. If he had not done that, it would not have happened." We see something on TV that is the result of someone's actions and say, "Look at that; that's what happens when people get involved in that." Avoid saying, "That is what will happen to you if you dare to do that."

Find every possible way to teach the 'law of consequences', both in the practical and theoretical. There is nothing that happens that does not have a consequence. Start talking about it when your children are very young. Talk about it to your partner when the children are present; talk about things that happened to you and the consequences that ensued, where you got it right and where you got it wrong and, most importantly, why. However, these conversations should be natural and part of everyday life, and not forced just so that we can get our point across. It is the consequences that come through our own decisions that we want to demonstrate. The children will begin to understand that things happen as a result of something else and they will pick up that some are good consequences and others are bad. To put it another way, they learn that some decisions are good and have a good outcome but other decisions are wrong and have a bad outcome. If we only start to teach this when our children reach their teen years it is too late and they will struggle when things get really difficult. The concept of consequences needs to be ingrained in them by the time they become teenagers because at that age our child will begin to want independence and think they can handle everything life throws at them. It gives our child understanding and strategies to better assess situations and in doing so avoiding conflict and unnecessary pain.

If we instil into our children the 'law of consequences' from infancy and it becomes established in them, even though it may seem to have vanished in their teen years, it will certainly re-emerge as they grow older and wiser. Consequences begin right from the start and continue through life – they never stop happening.

The concept here is not to create fear, which can happen if we are overprotective and cautious with everything. The 'law of consequences' is about developing the ability to assess the result of actions and take the consequences into account, mitigating them as much as possible and facing them square on. A man who climbs a mountain without understanding the danger is asking for trouble, but a man who assesses the dangers, plans for them and then climbs the mountain is practicing the 'law of consequences'.

What about the consequences of throwing stones? I was chatting to a friend about consequences and training children into good habits. She told me a story about her eldest son. His brothers told her that her eldest son was throwing stones. She went outside and told him this was wrong and he was to stop, and went back inside. The brothers came in later and told her that not only was he still throwing stones, but that he had broken a car headlight. She knew that he had to understand the consequences of his actions. Headlights cost money and he had money in the bank, so she found out how much a new headlight cost, took her son to the bank and drew out the cost of the new headlight. He cried all the way to the bank and all the way back because he did not want to lose any of his money. When she got home she put the money into an envelope and sent her son, by himself, to the neighbour to say sorry and pay for the headlight. He cried all the way. Later, the neighbour said to his mum, "Please don't ever put me through that again as it was so hard to see him like that." She just wanted to give the money back to him but that was the 'law of consequences' in action. That one instance would have had more impact on that boy than any other type of punishment.

There are many things in life that have serious consequences. Having the ability to look at both long and short-term outcomes can save our children from consequences that could ruin their lives. In a world with many dangers we owe it to our children to at least attempt to teach them this ability.

Chapter 15

The electronic world

Today we live in an electronic age. Interactive TV, smartphones, computers, tablets and computer games are all part of our lives. It is amazing to me to see a child as young as two years of age pick up their mum's smartphone, find some photos and begin to flick through them. Because these devices are such a part of everyday life, we parents need to learn how to use them confidently as well. I have observed two kinds of extremes in regard to the use of electronic gadgetry by young children. One family will restrict its use by having what is called 'screen time'. This means that the children are only allowed one hour per day watching or playing with anything involving a screen. Other families allow everything all the time. There are TVs and computers in bedrooms, children have smartphones, and electronic games are available at all waking times. Of course, there are many families who come in between these two extremes.

To get a perspective on this we need to ask what effect screens have on our children, should screen time be restricted, and if so, when and for how long? By their very nature screens are exclusive; that is, viewers have to concentrate on the screen and in doing so, exclude what or who is around them. It is primarily an individual pastime although it can sometimes involve a challenge with another player, although even then the child has to concentrate on their own screen in order to win the game or battle.

John Medina in his book, *Brain Rules for Babies* tells us, 'The fact is, the amount of TV a child should watch before the age of two is zero'. He also states, 'There is general agreement that a child's exposure to television of any type should be limited'. He continues, 'There is also general agreement that we are completely ignoring this advice'. (1) After two years of age he recommends limiting screen time to interactive programmes and that a parent should always be with the child during these times.

Evidently the best way to develop your child's brain is by spending a lot of time talking with them, using lots of 'face time'; that is real faces and not television faces[6].

The issue that we need to think about is the effect screens can have on our child's ability to interrelate with other children and adults. The question is; do they restrict the development of a child's ability to fully relate to others around them? When a child is under five, the amount of screen time may not be a major concern but we do need to consider it, because when a child reaches the age of four, hand-held, simple games can become all-consuming and distract them from play with others around them.

Let's switch away from electronics for a moment and think about play. Play has always been an important part of a child's development. When I was young it was Cowboys and Indians, or playing in a stream trying to dam it up. Other times it was making carts to race friends down hills, or making dens or tree houses to hide in. Play teaches children how to problem solve, develops their imaginations and makes them think up ways to entertain themselves. Play often involves other children so they learn how to develop relationships, negotiate, and acquire friendship skills while they play. We used to have playpens full of soft toys, balls and things which made various noises with which our children entertained themselves. When friends' children came around they all went in the playpen together and learned to interact with each other, not always harmoniously I have to say! This was all part of the process of learning how to get on with others; a necessary skill if they are to progress in life. It is easy to pop the TV on when there are other children around because then we do not have to deal with those little niggles that arise. However, it is in these little niggles that children learn to compromise, negotiate, come to an agreement and relate to one another; just as they will have to do when they start school.

Being from an older generation where electronics were not part of our family life, I have no personal experience of this, but I have watched how my own children and other close family friends have handled the issue. They have generally restricted screen time to short periods and have not allowed televisions or computers in bedrooms. When visitors are present the television and computer are switched off and handheld games are not played with unless permission is given to do so. The result is that the

6 Brain Rules for Baby – John Medina

children are aware of what is going on around them, and likely to be more sociable. I heard of a child who had a television in his bedroom. He was going to a sleepover and gave his parents a list of all the programmes he wanted recorded while he was away. Evidently they included all the 'soaps' and other rather dubious programmes his parents were unaware of. They were horrified that they did not know the type of programmes he was watching. He was, of course, older and in the middle years rather than the period we are dealing with here, but it does show that we need to have a plan in mind for the future. There is also the question of what we watch and participate in when using things like television, computers or games. The experts tell us that this has very little to do with how our lives develop. I query this as it seems to me that we are highly affected by what we view and participate in and what is going on around us. If somebody swears a lot around us then we pick up those words in our mind. I remember being concerned that certain swear words kept coming to my mind and then realised that this was quite understandable as I worked all day with people who swore a lot. When I left that environment the words gradually left my mind, but when I started to play golf and was again around people who swore a lot, those words began to return a little. If this is true for us as adults, how much more will it be for the young fertile minds of our under-fives?

My challenge is for us to think about what we want regarding our children and electronics, what effect it will have on our children, and what patterns of lifestyle it will draw them into. One family I know watches no television, but only DVDs. We need to think about those things, make a plan and stick to it, only adapting it as circumstances change, and then only when we have talked it through together to avoid uncertainty and inconsistency. One thing is certain – electronics, smartphones, TVs, tablets and computers are now an integral part of our lives. It follows that our children need to learn to use them, but we need to consider the balance between screens and the ability to relate to others as our children grow and develop.

It is important to remember that personal contact with family, friends and other children is very important in the development of our child's brain. Our child can only learn how to recognise different people and 'read faces' when they come in contact with real people; not through seeing people on screens or in pictures. In the early years it is vital for baby's development that personal contact is not replaced with screen time.

Chapter 16

Eating and exercise

What we eat is fundamental to our health and well-being, and therefore it is vital that our children are trained to eat a balanced diet that contributes to good health and vitality. We see the results of an unbalanced diet all around us. Obesity is one of the largest problems facing our children and young people. It is largely caused by an unbalanced diet of fast food, chips, fizzy drinks, snacks and sugar, together with a lack of exercise.

We need to ask ourselves; whose responsibility is it to control our child's diet? Is it the child's responsibility? If our child is allowed to eat whatever they like, whenever they like, do they have enough information or experience to make responsible choices? No; they cannot possibly be in a position to judge between choices because the general evidence is that they will more likely choose nothing but sweets and junk food. Junk food is deliberately designed to tempt our taste buds and make us want to eat more of it. If a child is brought up primarily on this type of diet, then this is what their body craves after and then woe betide us if they get a smell or sight of something that does not please them.

If it is not our child's responsibility to control their diet, then it can only be ours as parents. After all, they are in our care. We control what goes in our child's mouth and if they become obese there is a real possibility we have allowed them to become so. Children need to be trained in eating the right amount of the right foods and to be encouraged to get the right amount of exercise.

Let's start with what we as parents eat, because what we eat is what our children will eat. If we live on fast food so will our children, because our example is the basic training for their eating habits. Do we eat vast portions? Then that is our example to our child. If we eat a packet of biscuits in one go, then that is what we are teaching our child to do. If we eat multiple packs of chips, chocolate and sweets, consume fizzy drinks and visit fast food outlets regularly, then our children are being trained to do this also. That is life; just as our child will adopt our table manners and way of eating. It is advisable that we have a good look at our eating habits and consider the example we are setting and the effect this will have on our children.

The task is not always easy because children seem to have an inbuilt aversion to some foods. To look is to dislike, because children taste with their eyes and disliked foods never get past those eyes if they can help it. What is more, their aversions change all the time and can get worse as they grow older, as I have observed with my grandchildren who liked certain foods when young but then changed their minds when they became teenagers. Our two youngest granddaughters both ate curry when they were younger because it was their parents' favourite food. They then went through a stage of not wanting curry because it was too spicy but now they eat it again. Their dislikes never appear to be consistent, but it does not have to be like that, as many have proved over the years.

Now for the million-dollar question – How do we prevent our children from fussy or faddy eating and train them to eat well and comprehensively? I am writing this book based on experience and observation. I have two children and five grandchildren, and I have been a pastor for a long time and seen many families struggle with this issue. However, I have also seen many who have successfully trained their children to eat almost anything. What I am not is an expert on nutrition or on training children to eat, but the things I have seen, observed and experienced I would like to share with you. I also recommend that you read as much as you can on the subject[7]. I have observed that it is the parents' expectations that set the patterns for food and eating. Our own experience was that we had a basic expectation that was instinctive rather than researched. Like many, we had no teaching on the subject so we just got on with it. When I was at boarding school I had to eat everything on my plate or it came back at the next meal. (Yes, they would take it away and bring it back until you ate it.) This taught me to eat whatever was put before me and the fascinating thing was that I began to like everything. The treatment was harsh but it did help me realise that children could be trained to eat well. In our home we developed a rule for mealtimes – we

---

7 French Kids Eat Everything by Karen Billon

didn't have to eat all the food on our plate, but if we did not finish the main course then there was no pudding, sweets, biscuits or cake until the next main meal. This worked and our children quickly learnt to finish whatever was put before them.

Was our general ruling regarding food a good one? The evidence says that it possibly was not. It had the right result but it was a bit strict. For instance, our rule included having to eat stringy runner beans. We had gone on holiday once and the beans we grew had passed their best when we returned. However, we did not want to waste them and so we insisted that they all be eaten. Unfortunately, the result of this is that now both our children hate runner beans, so much so that our daughter decided that she was not going to use the same rules towards food with her own children. This rule was wrong because, while it encouraged the children to eat everything on their plates, which was good, it left no room for leaving some if they were feeling full – if we do go for the 'eat everything on your plate' rule, then we need to be very careful about portion size. I have watched with some concern when parents expect their children to eat meals far too big for their age. Contrast this with my friend's way of approaching the introduction of new foods that his children did not like the look of – if broad beans were on the menu then the children had to eat just one or two. They had to try at least everything on their plates but could leave the rest. There was no 'unless you eat that one broad bean there will be no pudding'. The expectation was that they try everything, even though they may have had to sit there for a while until they did.

Our children then, should eat what we eat and at least try everything on their plate. It does not matter how long they take to do it but we do not give way and we do expect them to eat a little of everything. We then celebrate with our children and they get the next course; we simply insist that everything in the main course should be at least tried before the next course comes out. It is the order of things. In this way we are teaching our child to try all foods. There will be some foods they will clearly not like and this became very obvious with our daughter who could not abide carrots. After a while we never made her even try them, and she does not eat them to this day. There is no doubt that there are foods that we do not like and will not eat, so why would we expect our children to like everything? However, they should try everything on their plate while they are finding out what they ultimately like and do not like, because some foods are an acquired taste. Children do not generally like Brussels sprouts, but unless they try them they will never acquire that taste. My children like Brussels sprouts because they had to eat them and acquired the taste. My friend's children like broad beans because they had to at least try them. It is advisable not to substitute foods or leave something off the plate because a child does not like what everyone else is having. If the child says they do not like peas, then just a few have to be eaten before pudding arrives. Everybody has the same, and everyone has to at least taste everything. It is a good idea to have family mealtimes with everyone sitting at the table until all have tried everything on their plates. Make it a chat and share-the-day time; make it fun. No TV, phones, electronics – it is family mealtime.

The web site www.goodnet.org[8] gives nine scientifically-proven benefits of eating together as a family:

1. Family dinners mean better family relationships.
2. Family meals lead to healthier food choices.
3. Eating as a family leads to better grades.
4. Family dinners are a chance to explore new foods.
5. Family dinners lead to greater happiness.
6. Homemade meals promote portion control.
7. Family dinners equal healthy kids.
8. Family dinners relieve stress.
9. Eating at home saves money.

The Collaborative Trust[9] has done research that indicates that eating together as a family has significant beneficial effects on binge drinking, smoking and suicidal thoughts during the teen years.

---

8 https://www.goodnet.org/articles/9-scientifically-proven-reasons-to-eat-dinner-as-family (December 2017)

9 http://collaborative.org.nz/ (December 2017)

We need to work out what our expectations are and stick to them, remembering that we are responsible for our children and what they eat is vital for their health and well-being.

When should we start? There is some evidence that when different foods are introduced at a very young age it is much easier for children to continue to try new things. Always remember that at different ages our children's tastes will change, and they will seek to get us to change our plan – but we need to stick with it.

Lastly, food intake should be combined with exercise. In today's busy world, we tend to go everywhere in the car or sit in front of a screen. We all need to walk, run and have some physical exercise, and the best thing we can do is to make this a family matter so that we all do it together.

Chapter 17

Rules or love?

I was brought up in a Shaftesbury Homes boarding school from the age of about five. I knew nothing of home life and rarely went home for holidays but spent them either at school or with foster parents. As I have been writing this I have been reflecting on the contrasts of my two lives – my experience at boarding school and my home life with Mary and our children.

When I think about boarding school, certain things stand out very distinctly. One is that I can never remember being cuddled or, for that matter, receiving any affection at all, but for one exception. There was a caretaker and his wife, Mr and Mrs Green, and I remember that these two dear folks did care but they were not permitted to show it openly, and were never able to give me a hug.

The other thing that stands out is that life was totally about rules. If you kept the rules then you existed without too much trouble from staff, even though there were some brutal teachers who just seemed to enjoy terrorising us. Our maths teacher used to have times table practice with a cane in his hand. He would then fire a question at a boy and if he did not answer in five seconds he was caned on the hand. I was so scared of that cane that I froze and could not answer the question, and so of course got caned. Another teacher loved to cane boys with their heads under a table. A female teacher delighted in making boys pull their trousers down and then spanking them with the back of a hair brush. I could go on but that gives you an idea of what life was like. These things generated fear; not love or security.

Another thing I remember was that everything was done by the bell. You got up when the bell rang, you washed when the bell rang, and you went to class when the bell rang. You went to dinner when the bell rang and you went to bed when the bell rang. What this regime produced in some boys was fear – just simple fear – which it did in me. In others it produced secretive rebellion and these boys became the school bullies, but of course the school code meant that you never told on anyone.

Why am I telling you this? Because this is not what family life is about! If you take the concepts outlined in this book and turn it into law, it will result in fear or rebellion, or possibly children who are compliant at home but horrors outside it. Law requires rules to be obeyed and just like my boarding school, punishment is the only result if the rules are not kept.

Yes, we are training our children for adulthood but they should never know that this is what you are doing. Law and rules are like a standard which we must keep. To step outside the rules is to invoke punishment and generate failure, or, to put it another way, they are codes of behaviour against which we have to measure ourselves – and guess what? We often fail and that is no way to live.

Our children are never given a curriculum that explains what is needed to graduate into adulthood. They never sit an exam to prove their competence before they can move on to the middle years at the age of five or to the teen years at around twelve or thirteen. Our child transfers from one stage to the next regardless of what we have allowed them to become. It is, then, our responsibility to help them grow and mature to be emotionally and mentally ready for the next stage of their life. Our work is seen in the resulting characteristics of our children. However, it is not automatic because ultimately it relies on our child to respond. In the end they can decide to go their own way and we must accept that. Our job is to give them the best possible start and the best possible example to follow.

The prevailing atmosphere must be love and not fear. An example of how incidents can affect people can be seen in an experience my son had when young which had a powerful effect on him. Evidently, I was sitting on the sofa cuddling up with his sister when he tried to join in and I said, "Boys don't need to cuddle up, that's for girls." He never forgot that incident and felt that it deprived him of knowing my affection. I was mortified and assured him that I was truly sorry and loved him very much, and of course gave him a big hug then and there. Having been through an environment of fear at boarding school, I was determined that my children were not going to go through the same. I did not know how to be a good parent but I did know that I did not want fear to be a part of their upbringing. In my eyes our family was a unit that belonged together. It was cemented by love and our role as parents was to bring our children safely to adulthood. We have remained close even though at the time of this writing, half the family are living in New Zealand and half are in the UK. We trust one another and as parents and grandparents Mary and I are respected by our families.

Parenting is not easy, in fact it is anything but easy. We are dealing with a child's personality with its own disposition – and for that reason alone we must avoid cloning. We are not trying to reproduce ourselves. Our child may have quite a different personality from our own but we must find ways of understanding and encouraging that difference. However, having said that, who we are will rub off on our child and we will, at some stage, see ourselves in him or her; but it is important that we do not try to gain fulfilment through our child. For example, a dad wants to be a great rugby player but certain circumstances prevent him from doing so. The temptation is for him to seek to fulfil his dream through his son. So, every moment from the time his son can walk, the dad throws a rugby ball at him, encouraging him to love the sport as much as he does. This is fine if his son genuinely loves it, but if he doesn't and would rather be playing an instrument or reading a book, while dad is saying, "No, you are a boy and rugby is the only thing there is in life for a boy," then the dad is potentially suppressing the boy's natural ability. We should support the things we see in our child and encourage them.

The early years are about our children forming character and developing attributes that are common to mankind – respect, honesty, giving and integrity. To succeed we will need to love our children from the heart. We will need to put their interests before our own. One day my son asked me, "Dad, why is it that you go without if there are only three pieces of cake left?" – I was able to teach him about what it means to be the man of the family by putting the welfare of the other members before himself.

To succeed we will also need to understand the character traits that are helpful for our children as they relate to others around them – again respect, honesty, giving and integrity. If we don't understand it then neither will they. We will need to demonstrate these attributes in our own lives – we dare not say one thing and then do another. We may think that our under-five-year old is not aware of how we are, but beware, they might not be able to articulate what they see and hear but they are taking it all in. We need to be consistent in what we say and demonstrate what we teach by action. Confused messages will confuse our children. Does 'no' really mean 'no' or does it really mean 'maybe' or even 'yes' after a bit of nagging?

Let me assure you that we will never get it all right and that's okay! Parenting is not an exact science because it relies on the cooperation of our children. We know not all children are easy, as with the three-year-old who declared that she did not want to be a child and then spent the whole of her childhood trying to gain independence and be an adult. Is that easy? Of course not; we have to hold on and because we love, we will not let go.

What must be avoided is our child becoming the one in control who dictates how the family is run, what the family will do and when it will be done; or worse, when one parent has to stay with a child because they just do not want to do what the rest of the family is doing. Sometimes it is tough but if the family is doing it, we all do it without exception.

Do not confuse love with giving in all the time. We should seek to understand what it is we want to see in our five-year-old who is about to start school and work toward it with all the love we can muster; being consistent, but not harsh and abounding in love.

Earlier in this chapter I explained that our children will not understand what we are trying to achieve in them. The Bible describes it as putting hedges in place that guide them in the way that is set before them. There are consequences when our children step outside the hedges because they are there to help them stay within the boundaries set for them. However, love must always be the motivating factor; the hedges are our love for our children that protects, nourishes and guides them and our objective is for these hedges to become so inherent in our children that they will eventually choose these safe paths for themselves. When Mary and I saw the baby who just would not stay in bed our reaction was, 'That is just not going to happen with our children'. It was not because we wanted an easy life, but because we loved our children and wanted the best for them, and part of this was for them to get enough sleep so they could develop and learn. As they grew older we removed that hedge because it was no longer needed.

Our children don't know what is right and what is wrong, so it is our responsibility to put the hedges in place for their safety and development. Love, not rules, must be our motivation.

Chapter 18

Preparing for school

By the age of four our child will be active both in speech and physical activity and we will be considering what school we will enrol them in.

When one of our granddaughters was at this stage her parents began to consider these questions; should they teach her to read and write, and what about numbers? They were considering buying a computer programme to kick-start her education, preparing her for school. They did not know if it was advantageous for her to get a head start and if that would make it any easier for her, so they decided to ask a friend of the family, who was a head teacher, for his thoughts. He advised them that it was relatively easy for a teacher to teach reading, writing and numbers, but what a child needed was plenty of experiences, lots of play and good imagination. In addition to this, there were other things that made starting school easier for children and he recommended that children should be able to dress themselves, tie their own shoelaces and be familiar with standing, sitting and knowing their 'left', 'right', and 'up' and 'down'. This made a lot of sense because they would not be needing the teacher's attention all the time for help in these areas. Evidently it is common for children starting school not to be able to accomplish these things, and it can be quite a problem for school staff.

One of the things that schools require is for the child to be able to sit and work at something. It may be that a child only has to sit still and concentrate for fifteen minutes at a time but this can be a problem for some children. If a child is active and needing stimulation from somebody else all the time, this can be difficult when they are suddenly required to sit and concentrate while at school. I have observed during church meetings that some families work at getting their children to concentrate by having them join in with the first couple of songs and then allowing them to draw or read. Other children are allowed to roam around while others demand their parents' attention all the time and will make a fuss if they don't. I am not passing judgement but merely stating my observations with the thought that it is advantageous for our child to be able to sit and concentrate without constant attention when they start school. If we understand this we will put some effort into training our children to be able to sit and concentrate when required.

Another possible advantage is the ability to keep things tidy and in order. One of the constant battles my two children had with their own children was keeping the children's rooms clear of clutter and tidy. As I have watched this over the years I have wondered what would happen if a child was taught to put things away after use and to keep things tidy from the start. Of course, initially it would be the parents doing it with the child; maybe picking up one or two things with them but then as the child got older they would become more and more responsible for putting their things away.

The last area in which we can prepare our children for school is in their social interaction with other children and adults. If a child cannot interact and share with other children, they can quickly become isolated when in a crowd of their peers. In the same way, if the only adults a child interacts with are their parents, then they are going to have difficulty relating to teachers who are new to them. We have to be careful with whom our children relate but there are many adults in a typical family circle, and within safe parameters, that we should encourage our children to have conversations and safe play with. There are families I visit where I play and have great fun with their under-fives.

Our child is about to enter the next phase of childhood; the middle years. Everything we have been seeking to put into our child must carry on into this next phase of their life. Character is still being formed and school opens up all manner of challenges of which we need to be aware. We will revisit many of the ideas explored for these early years and expand our thinking as our child grows in knowledge, confidence and experience during the middle years.

Chapter 19

What do we want to see when our child is five years old?

How would you answer somebody who asked you, "What would you ideally like your child to be like at five years of age?" Five is a crucial age because from that time a massive change takes place and the journey to independence begins – very slowly at first, but the reality is that powerful influences other than your own will begin to push into your child's life. It is not just school; it is also peer pressure, teachers and the possibilities of independent actions.

At five years of age, the character traits that are to govern our lives are being nurtured. The hope is that respect, honesty, trustworthiness and integrity with generosity are being established in our child. They will not, of course, be fully established, but enough to be visible. What are the indicators we want to see in our child that tell us we are succeeding in our endeavours and that they (and we) are doing okay? Here are some suggestions which may help clarify our thinking:

1. Has our child got to the point where they know what is right or wrong and we can trust them? Here is an example – recently we were out driving and came to a Give Way sign. As we reached the intersection, two little boys, who I estimate were around four years of age, came up to the kerb on their bikes, stopped and began to talk to each other. I immediately wondered if they were on their own as no adults seemed to be near them. Then I noticed two mums with pushchairs about one hundred metres behind them. They obviously trusted the boys to stop until they caught up with them. It seemed to me that the boys knew that the kerb was their limit and they were waiting for their mums to see them across the road. Would that have just happened? I would suggest

that there would have been much training prior to this, and there would have been quite a few trials along the way!

2. Is our child polite to visitors and family members? We recently visited some friends in Perth, Australia. We were greeted warmly by the two daughters of the house, who were a little over five. They politely asked if we were okay after our flight from New Zealand and generally chatted to us very happily. When I had a moment, I asked the parents if the children's friendliness came naturally or whether they had had to work at getting the girls to be polite to visitors and family. They smiled and told us of the time they went to a family gathering and one of the girls refused to say anything to anyone. The mum was having none of it and told her daughter that if she was going to be rude by being impolite then they would not stay. Even though the child cried because she did not want to go home, they went home and left the rest of the family to enjoy the get-together. That lesson and many other incidents had taught the girls to respond to those around them.

3. Does our child have a basic honesty about them? Can we see that our child owns up when things have gone wrong or do they try to hide the truth from us?

4. Does our child tell us about problems before we ask?

5. Does our child go to bed without fighting us every inch of the way and when they are in bed, do they go to sleep?

6. Is our child helpful and do they clear up after play? I was with a family who had three children and I noticed an incident where some toys were on the floor beside a play table. Dad pointed them out to the little boy and indicated that they should not be there. The young child continued to walk away but was firmly, without being shouted at, asked to put them where they belonged. The lad looked at his dad and came back and picked them up without argument. I could see that this must have been

something the parents had worked on with their son; that when you get things out, you also put them back. I remember the time a family came to visit our home. The children were rather unruly. Out came the Lego and all the toys from the toy box were spread over the floor. When the time came for them to go, Mary simply got down on her knees and said, "Come on now, let's put all this away together." Their mum was dumbfounded when all three of her children, who never put anything away at home, meekly put everything back into the toy box. Why did they do that when they never did it at home? Because Mary expected it and was not going to accept a 'no'. Somehow those children were aware of this and just got on and did it with her.

7. Does our child display a general obedience where the situation arises where we have to say, 'stop' or 'no'? Why 'general'? Because most children living with loving parents will at some time try to push the limits set for them. It's normal, and the result of a developing personality where we as parents are teaching them to think for themselves. Our child is not a puppet, but a living, thinking human who is being trained for adulthood. Our child needs to be free to express themselves and to push the boundaries within a loving home environment. Having a little discussion every now and again with pleas and explanations does no harm. However, they also need to know that a 'no' will not become a 'yes', whereas a 'maybe' might go either way. It is good, occasionally, to let our child influence our decision before we say that final 'no'. We can say, "okay, just this once."

I was on an aeroplane and a mum with three children, between the ages of three and six years of age had one seat next to me and three across the aisle. One lad came and dived into the seat next to me but his mum pointed to the three seats, indicating that that was where he was to sit.

"Aw mum, I want to sit here!"

"Over the other side," she said.

"But Mum!"

She just looked and pointed and over he went. He could have protested because he had a good relationship with his mum, but in the end, he did as he was told.

If there is no wriggle room for children to push the limits, it may indicate that the atmosphere at home is too rigid. By rigid I mean that rules must be obeyed without question and the consequences may be too harsh. This can happen with the best of intentions but unfortunately, the result can be fear rather than the contentment that a loving atmosphere generates. Fear makes children close up and they then tend to create other outlets for that normal pushing of boundaries or the need to express frustration. This can result in a child becoming an angel at home but a horror outside the home during the middle years. On the other hand, this can also happen if our child is pampered and indulged and becomes the centre of the household. In this case, the result can be a spoilt child who does not rock the boat at home but later becomes a potential bully outside the home.

Let me explain this by telling you the story of Tony (not his real name) who was about eight or nine years old and in my Sunday school class. He was arrogant, rude and threatened violence. Once when I had to ask him to leave Sunday school, he used every swear word I ever knew, and before I became a Christian I was a prolific user of swear words! I just thought he was a troubled kid and probably had a terrible home life. One day we went on a Sunday school outing to the south coast of England. We travelled in two coaches but on the way home we had a serious crash. Fortunately, no one was injured but we did need to wait for two replacement coaches to take us home. This meant that we would be arriving home very late and so we rang one of the church leaders to let the parents know what had happened, that everyone was okay and to give them an approximate time of arrival. When we got back I noticed Tony's mum come to get him and was amazed at the reaction from both of them – His mum cried, "My baby, I was so worried!" and this went on and on for some time, while Tony was a passive, whimpering mess, sobbing, "Mummy, I was so frightened." You can imagine – I just stood there with my mouth wide open at this lad who was so vicious when away from home but so highly-strung and pampered by his mother.

I don't know why it is like that, but I do know that I have learnt to fear when children are 'angels' at home because they are often the opposite when away from home. Had Tony learnt that bad behaviour outside the home was the way to get attention, and that argument or opposition to his parents at home resulted in harsh punishment? Is this why he was compliant at home but a bully outside the home? We will never know, but whatever the reason, this is something to guard against with our own children.

What I like to see is a child who at home has a little spirit and will push the limits but will be compliant when the chips are down. One of my granddaughters often argues the point at home, eventually doing as she is asked, but outside the home, she is known for her manners and kindness towards others.

Think about what it is that you would like to see in your child at the age of five. In chapter 6 I said that it is in these early years when character is being formed. The dictionary defines character as, 'The combination of traits and qualities distinguishing the individual nature of a person; reputation, especially a good one'.

To reiterate from Chapter 6, we would say that the three foundational character traits we would like to see established in our five-year-old are honesty, good manners and generosity. We expanded on these pillars and said that honesty is respect for other people's views, dignity and property, that being polite signals that we care about how others feel, and that giving indicates a willingness to help. In each of our families we have expectations of each other. It is into these cultural settings that we introduce our new family member and we train them in the ways of our society and family.

These character traits are what we should be seeing in our five-year-old. Yes, there is a long way to go and much still to learn, and all the training that has been going on has to continue on into the next chapter of our child's life. However, we still need to be in control and we certainly cannot let go now.

Parents often wonder where their children pick up the concepts that govern their lives. You know the sorts of things – knowing what is right or wrong, knowing how to treat other people and their possessions, and having a good work ethic that will help determine how successful they will be in life. We particularly wonder where bad habits and naughtiness come from. Do you notice how we never have to teach our child to be naughty? There seems to be a built-in instinct in many to kick against authority. Take the mum who told me that when her daughter was about three years old she suddenly said, "Mummy, I don't want to be a child, I want to be an adult." Her mum told me that from that moment on she was a difficult child and that as parents they had to hold on hard and refuse to let her go her own way. She was not going to gain her independence until she became an adult. It was hard work at times but they persevered and today she is a stable and well-adjusted adult. What would have happened if her parents had given into her three-year-old's desire? Of course, we cannot guarantee that outcome every time, but we owe it to our children to try.

We are concentrating here on the period before school – a long way from graduation into adulthood. However, it is important to keep the end result in view, which is adulthood, not childhood.

These early years are a wonderful time, both for us and our children. Enjoy these years as they pass so quickly; they are to be cherished and made the most of because they are of the utmost importance in laying the foundation for the years to come. But much more than that, they are about love and the establishing of a relationship that will hopefully be fruitful long after our child reaches adulthood and has established their own family. There is still a long way to go. But consider that in another thirteen years our child will be doing final exams at school ready to launch out into university and life beyond home. The foundations for that are largely laid in these first five years.

Part Two

The Middle Years

Caution

If you are reading this during pregnancy or within two years of your child's birth, I suggest that put this aside for now. Pick the book up again when your child is three to four years old and read the "Middle Years". The reason for this suggestion is that it is enough to concentrate on the 'Early Years' without thinking ahead before necessary.

Introduction to the Middle Years

Caution – Adults in training

Five years have been spent seeking to form good character in your child. That task is not yet finished and will continue right through the middle years. Character is consolidated under pressure. What will be different once your child turns five is that other influences are going to enter their life. School and the influence of teachers coupled with peer pressure will all challenge your child's character at some time. During this period, it should never be forgotten that your child's security and stability are rooted in home and within the relationship of their family – hold on to that family relationship and counter anything negative that seeks to push your child in a different direction.

As I have observed the families around me and, of course, the families of my two children with their children, I have noticed that there are certain friction points. These create tension in both parents and children and often result in irritable moods, anger and resentment on the part of the child and frustration for the parents.

Common friction areas:

- Tidiness
- Bedtimes
- Homework
- Electronics
- Money
- Eating

As children get older there are also:

- Alcohol/drugs
- Sex/pornography

As I have been writing this book I have been doing a lot of thinking about these areas. Does it have to be like this? Can we mitigate the frustration brought on by these areas?

My thoughts are based on observing those parents who make it work and those who struggle, and I'm fascinated by the proverb that has inspired this book – 'Train up a child in the way he should go; even when he is old he will not depart from it'. (Proverbs 22:6)

This proverb tells us that it is the parents' responsibility to train their children for the adult world, and that this training will result in lifelong habits. Of course, it will seem a battle at times, and of course, our children will kick against our parental efforts on occasions. But is that any reason not to do the very best we can for our children in preparing them for the adult world?

I have observed that a lot of success in parenting can be put down to the expectation of the parents. If we do not expect something to happen it generally will not, but if we expect it to happen it generally will, even though there will always be struggles from time to time. Parents who have always expected their children to get on with things usually experience a minimum of fuss.

Another observation is that human beings operate on learnt patterns. If you tie your shoelaces in a certain fashion, the chances are you will always do it that way. My son-in-law has a very strange way of tying his laces but it is the way he learnt to do it and so that is the way he does it. Of course, it is not strange to him; it is only strange to us watching him. To successfully play golf the player needs what is called muscle memory – training the brain to automatically swing the club. If you think too much about what you are doing it just does not work. (I obviously think about my swing too much!) Learnt patterns are true in these practical areas and are also true in the emotional areas of our lives.

During the Christchurch earthquakes, when parents expressed fear and even panic, their children often exhibited the same patterns, whereas when parents reacted with fortitude and courage in the face of fear, their children usually followed. After the February 22nd earthquake, I asked my youngest granddaughter if she was scared. She replied, "No it was great fun!" Her parents had said to her, "Wow, just think, you will be able to tell your children you were in the Christchurch earthquakes!" All of us who experienced the earthquakes suffered fear and panic to some extent, but some suffered much more than others and yet kept a positive attitude, and this rubbed off on their children. Positive recovery was what brought us back to normality.

As we explore the chapters ahead we will learn how to continue to impart life-governing principles to our children. If those principles are consistent and well established, then it will be more difficult for them to be changed by new, outside influences.

By the time our child reaches five years of age, their character is largely formed but it is still vulnerable to outside influences. We will explore these new influences which include school life, playground culture and peer pressure. Children are a great joy and it is our privilege to guide them into adulthood.

Chapter 20

Consolidating Character

We have been building character into our children and we should be seeing this by now in their behaviour and conduct toward those they come in contact with. Even at five years of age children will have a reputation with those around them based on how they act. There is a proverb that confirms this by telling us that, 'Even small children are known by their actions, so is their conduct pure and upright'.

One way to find out their reputations is to ask good friends or teachers who know the children outside the home.

I well remember going for a parent-teacher interview regarding our very young son and the teacher putting her head in her hands and beginning the conversation with, "What on earth are we going to do with Martin?" My reaction was immediate and decisive; "If he is causing trouble, please tell us about it and I will deal with it." You see, I wanted to know what he was like outside the home so I could correct any disrespect or dishonesty. It was important to me that I was made aware of anything of concern so I could correct any character faults that were developing in him. Martin's teacher was horrified to think she had led us to believe Martin had behavioural issues. The problem was not that at all but that he would often daydream in class – one day when she saw him sitting staring out of the window at a plain brick wall, and obviously not hearing a word she was saying, had asked, "What do you see, Martin?" "A spaceship," he replied. She then went on to tell us that he was a lovely, helpful child and a pleasure to be around. We could tell from this the type of reputation Martin had with others and encouraged us that we were on the right track.

In an ideal world, basic characteristics at the age of five would hopefully include; (in embryo form) respect, honesty, integrity, trustworthiness and loyalty, together with a general generosity of spirit.

At the age of five, our children have only finished the first stage of the development of their characters. It is a platform that can be built on and is tested by the pressure cooker of life outside of our parental control. For this reason, the ages from birth to five are crucial. In the early years we looked at the proverb, 'Train up a child in the way he should go; even when he is old he will not depart from it'. This sets the objective; preparing the children for adulthood, and this is still the parental objective for the middle years from the ages of five to thirteen. New influences are now entering the scene, but it is still our responsibility and objective as parents to bring our children to adulthood in the best possible condition, and that means continued development of character. After the middle years, the drive for independence begins in earnest, and at that point, it is very difficult to change any negative characteristics that may have crept in.

At five years of age children do not wake up with every characteristic that has been instilled in them, and which is magically set in place for evermore. They still cannot understand all that is happening; they still cannot figure out what life is all about, but they are becoming more aware of what is going on around them and the vast array of possibilities life has to offer them.

Let me give you a couple of examples – Television advertisements played during children's programmes seek to awaken the 'I want' desire for things. The 'I want' desire can lead to selfishness in our children, and if allowed, will cut across the principle of sharing and therefore kindness being instilled in them. Children are very sensitive and because these characteristics are not fully formed in them they can be 'blown off course'. Take the example of the little four-year-old girl who quite happily shared with others at the childminder's home she had been attending since a baby. One day her cousin came to live in the district and he was a grabbing, 'It's mine!' kind of child. This influenced the little girl to the extent that she began to grab things from the other children at the childminder's home with the exclamation, "It's mine." Fortunately, the childminder knew how to deal with situations like this. She took the toy off the little girl and said something like, "No it's not yours, it's mine, but you can borrow it if you will share it with the others; if not, you cannot play with it." She was reinforcing the generosity of spirit that had been fostered by her parents but that had been challenged by her cousin's example. We cannot slacken off on the character training that began in the early years. Rather, we need to hold onto these principles and see them mature in our children.

To help understand what is happening, look at the illustration at the end of this chapter. There are parallel hedges put in place in the early years, where parents are in control and children learn basic obedience; by that I mean they know mum and dad are in charge and they need to respond to them. Between these hedges is the safe place where mum and dad hold all the responsibility. From around the age of five, the hedges begin to widen out – if they didn't (because children are developing human beings), this would create frustration. To develop into adults children need to learn to think for themselves and make decisions within the hedges that have been put in place by mum and dad. For instance, those character traits we keep mentioning (honesty, integrity, trustworthiness and loyalty, together with a general generosity of spirit), are generally non-negotiable and reinforced by parents, as is obedience when it is required.

Notice in the illustration that parents are depicted as 'holding on'. Any parent who has gone through this stage will confirm this. When my friend's child announced at the age of three that she wanted to be an adult and not a child, she tried everything she could to gain control from her parents. Her parents would not allow it – they literally 'held on' to her until she reached the time they needed to let go. They did let go eventually and as a result of their 'holding on' she developed into a very stable adult, who now has a very good relationship with her parents. What about a young child I knew whose parents described him as 'hell on two legs'? How easy it would have been for his parents to let go and not bother because the task was too hard. They declared, 'He will not win, we will not let him go'. He also turned out to be a fine and stable young man. As parents, we need to be determined not to let go but at the same time be flexible enough to allow our children to begin making decisions for themselves when appropriate. Choosing their style of dress (providing, of course, they are not inappropriate) can be an area where our children can gradually decide for themselves.

Notice that the description for the child in the illustration is 'flexing muscles', because that is what children do as they grow older, and it should be expected. The older the children get, the more say they will want in controlling their own lives. They do not yet have the life skills to know how to handle all the situations they will come up against – those positive characteristics of respect, honesty, integrity, trustworthiness and loyalty, together with generosity, are not yet fully formed in them, and our task of instilling these will continue until around the age of thirteen, depending on the child. This is why the parenting label in the illustration is 'holding on'. The illustration also shows the final stage, which for parents is letting go. For our children, the middle years are a time of gaining confidence while still within the wider hedges set by us as parents. This allows our children to learn how to practise making their own decisions in a safe and secure environment – we will discuss this stage in the final section of this book, 'The Teen Years'.

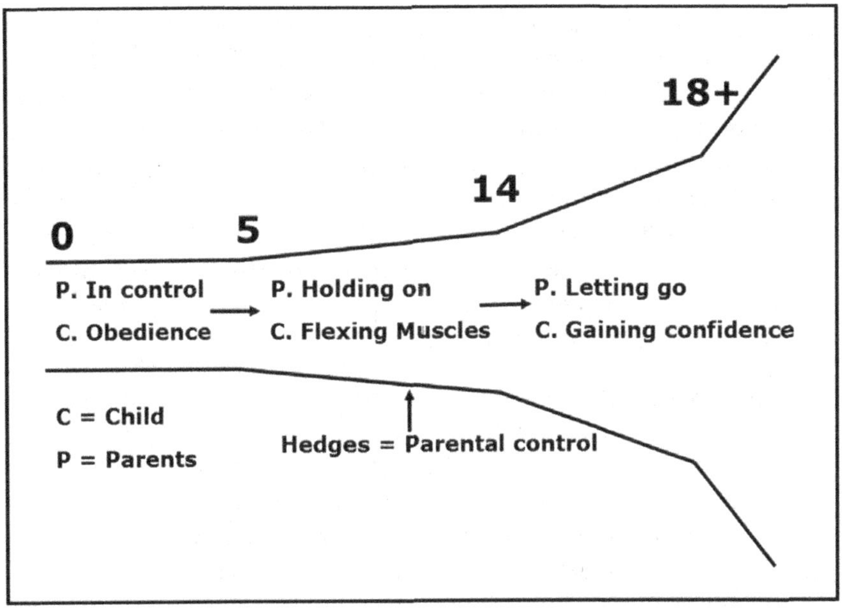

Figure 1

Chapter 21

Open Communication

Most children today will have spent some time at preschool, with a childminder or kindergarten. In some ways, this will have helped prepare them for school because they would have had to learn to relate and play with other children. However, early education is different from school in that the children are very young, the staff ratios are high and learning is mainly done through play. School means being in a class of 25-30 children with one teacher and possibly, but not always, a class helper. It also means open playtime with some supervision but at nowhere near the levels of preschool or kindergarten. Some children are only in childcare or kindergarten part-time, whereas school is full-time.

Here are some interesting statistics – there are 24 hours in a day and 168 hours in a week. In a normal school day, assuming our children go to bed at around seven each evening and get up at seven the next morning, they sleep for 12 hours or 50% of the day. Assuming they spend five and a half hours at school, it means they are only under our direct influence 27% of any school day and only 33% of any week during term time.

School Day	Week
Sleep 7 pm to 7 am = 50%	84 hours = 50%
School 5 days 5.5 hours = 23%	27.5 hours = 17%
With parents 6.5 hours = 27%	56.5 hours (including weekend) = 33%

At school our children are placed in an environment with different influences for 23% of the day. We need to consider those influences and help our children understand how to cope with both the environment and the influences that will be a part of their lives for the rest of their childhood.

This school environment can be for them either good, bad or anything in between. Home is their secure world, their main anchor in life – it has been the centre of their world to date, the place where they can express themselves, the place where their possessions are, and the place where they belong. For the new school child, it is vital that when they return home they can offload what has been happening in this other world of school. The parents' task at this point is to listen, with very little interruption and with no lecturing or expressing doubt about what is being said. Children need the confidence to express themselves without immediate correction, interjection, doubt and especially without lectures. A 'wow', a 'really', an 'ah' or even a 'goodness me' are acceptable because the children need to be able to express themselves freely.

The following story, made available by *Care for the Family (UK)*, from their course 'Positive Parenting' illustrates the point. It is entitled *Two sides of the story.*

From the daughter

'At 11 or 12, I asked my mum what she'd do if I started smoking. She said, "I'd throw you out of the house!" I did try it – only to look big – but I felt I couldn't tell her then. But now I'm happy to talk about anything with her – boys, cigarettes, drink.

We get on so well now but, looking back, there were times I felt she didn't listen. I remember when I was really little, being at the house of a friend of hers. I kept saying, "Mum, I need the loo." But she was too engrossed in conversation to hear. In the end, I wet myself. I felt so ashamed, I was crying – and Mum was upset, too, because she hadn't listened to me. She said, "I'm so sorry. In future, I will listen." That made me feel much

From the mother

'When my daughter shouted, "You never listen to a word I say!" I was completely shocked. I felt I'd spent the 13 years of her life listening to her! But she said, "You listen, but you never hear me." The more I thought, the more I realised she was right. If she came home from school, upset about something someone had said to her, I'd say, "There, there – I'm sure he didn't mean it." I'd try to make her feel better by denying what she was better. After that things did improve, but I think she still tended to think about what she wanted, not what I wanted. And she'd try to sort things out when I didn't want them to be sorted out.

saying instead of acknowledging her feelings.

I'd quite often ask something innocently and be given huge amounts of information. It was exasperating. There'd be useful bits in there somewhere, but I got bored listening.

When she was very young she would often ask me quite searching questions – such as why flies got stuck in spiders' webs but spiders didn't. I was excited that she was bright and inquisitive, so if I didn't know the answer I'd make a project for us to find out. In the end, she stopped asking questions. She was too young for all the information I was flooding her with.

I've always valued lots of things about my Mum, though, and a couple of years ago I felt a change in her. She went to classes about parenting and seemed more able to listen to me, so we could talk through our differences instead of having a slanging match. We get on really well now.'

In later years, after accusing me of not listening, I went to parenting skills classes, which were a real eye-opener. I learnt how to see her point of view.

I think we communicate brilliantly now. She may be my daughter, but she's also her own person with her own opinions and feelings, which I respect. By imposing mine on her, we both missed out. Since I started listening – and hearing – I've met a different person, a wonderful young woman.'

If children stop expressing themselves to their parents it becomes very difficult to know what is going on within them or around them. Some children are talkers and others are not. You know the kind of thing – they come home from school and you ask, "Had a good day?" and all you get is "Yep". That's okay, provided that when there is a problem and the time is right for them, they will open up. Our children will only talk to us if we show them we are really interested in what they are saying. We can do this by giving good eye contact and involving them in the solution – even a whiff of distraction can kill off the desire to communicate and result in withdrawal from our child.

One of the skills our children will need as adults is the ability to think through problems, find a solution and put it into action. Included in this is the ability to converse with other people in order to get a broad spectrum of ideas. As parents, we can be teaching them how to do this from an early age. We will see in later chapters, that school brings pressure and pressure requires the ability to problem-solve. If every problem is solved for them they will just sit back and let it happen, but when adulthood comes they will lack the skills to do it for themselves. My granddaughter had a problem at school. There was a girl with Asperger's Syndrome in her class and my granddaughter and her friends often played with her. Unfortunately, from time to time this girl caused trouble. In previous years they'd had a teacher who understood the situation and would take the girl aside – the teacher understood that the others were not the problem but that they were simply trying to help. However, the next year they had a new teacher who knew nothing of this history. One day this girl started a fight and the girls (as they had always done before), tried to break it up and calm her down. Unfortunately, they were all brought before the teacher who gave them a severe telling-off for fighting and banned them from their favourite lunchtime place in the playground. My granddaughter was extremely upset as she felt she had been misunderstood and she hated getting into trouble. How could this be solved? My granddaughter talked to her parents, other family members and us to find a solution. My daughter went to see the teacher but that, sadly, had very little result. In the end, our granddaughter came up with the solution herself. She went to the girl involved, explained that she would not be playing with her all the time but just a couple of times a week, and when trouble broke out, our granddaughter moved to another part of the playground. Through discussion and strategising with the family, my granddaughter was able to find a solution for her problem, which she put into action successfully. If she hadn't been comfortable enough to tell her parents about her problem, they would not have been able to help and guide her into finding a solution for herself.

All this is training for adult life; we as parents provide security for our children as we support and enable them to find solutions to the pressures they encounter. After listening (without too much comment!) to our children, there may well be things that need attention or correction but we need to bring those things up in conversation without trying to tackle them head-on. Later on, maybe at bed time, start the conversation with, "You know you said ... what do you think is ...?" or "Do you think that was right and if not, why?" This can be done without undermining our child, and in this way, we are training them in the skills they will need as an adult. We are vital in helping our child develop sound judgment that will help them find the solutions to the problems they will come up against both now and later in life.

Laying the foundation for good decision-making is one of the keys to a stable and happy life. Bad decision-making results in negative situations which, in turn, result in a stressful and unhappy life. Children need to learn that the consequences they experience are the result of the choices they make. The key is teaching them that whether they are good at making decisions or not, the best way to avoid making bad decisions is consultation with those they trust.

This naturally leads to the consideration of options. There are always options, and it is the consideration of these options that leads to making good decisions. A way of assessing options is to note the positives and the negatives, or for our child, what's good and what's bad, about an action. As the objective is to help our child think for themselves, gentle prompting or suggestions are wise.

Questions to ask:

- What are the options in this situation?
- What benefits come from each option?
- What negative consequences come from each option?
- Are you willing to accept the consequences?
- What personal values are involved in this decision?
- What are you going to do, and do you need help to do it?

This can be started at a very early age, but lecturing, pressuring and too much information are to be avoided. Questions need to be simple and conversational in style. As our child learns to read and write they can be encouraged to write down the options. Encouraging them to do this each time a difficult situation arises can hopefully help prevent them from making bad decisions later on in life.

There are two more questions to encourage our child to ask:

- How will I feel afterwards?
- How will the people I value feel about me after this decision/action?

In this way, our child is being trained to assess the options and make good decisions right throughout their lives. This is a major lesson in life and can only be achieved if the communication between us as parents and our child is not shut down early in childhood, usually from the failure of not listening and taking our children seriously.

This quote from the writer and lecturer, Catherine M. Wallace, is a good way to finish this chapter.

'Listen earnestly to anything your children want to tell you, no matter what. If you don't listen eagerly to the little stuff when they are little, they won't tell you the big stuff when they are big, because to them all of it has always been big stuff'.

Chapter 22

School

Our children are entering a new environment which will become a large part of their lives. Chapter 21 outlined the importance of keeping open communication with our children during this time. This is crucial because from the time our children start school, they begin to become more independent and it is essential to know the decisions they are making and the actions being taken. The first five years have been preparing our children for this. We have instilled in them a sense of respect for others and enabled them to relate both to other children and to adults. This is important when they find themselves in a classroom with an adult teacher and thirty other children.

School brings with it the possibility of independent action because you as parents are not there to guide or challenge. Let's examine a few of the possibilities:

1. Choice

Their teacher may be experienced or new to the job. There will be good teachers and not so good teachers, but one thing is certain – they will not have the same view of your children as you do. Children have to earn their teacher's respect because it doesn't come automatically and is directly related to the respect and attention they give in response to the teacher. Teachers are human beings who are doing the job of educating children. It is impossible for them to give a great deal of individual attention to every child.

The class situation involves developing the concentration and listening skills of every individual child in that class. In the early years children are encouraged to sit and concentrate in preparation for the school years. They learnt at home, preschool or day-care to concentrate and relate to other children and adults. These skills, or the lack of them, either disable or enable the children to take in what is being taught by the teacher. This, then, is the first point of independent action – the choice to listen, or not to listen, to the teacher, the choice to concentrate and learn, or the choice to play up and be distracted. Even though I have heard it said by many pupils that they thought their teachers had eyes in the back of their heads, our children still have to choose to take notice.

Education is vital to every child's future as an adult. It provides the means by which the child has options where they have the ability to choose, and the ability to consider and choose an action or direction. Education has the power to give options – For example, the greater number of exam subjects passed opens up a greater number of career options available in the adult world. It starts right here in the first year of school life, but the platform for it is laid in the early years before school.

Let me give you an example – A young man, who wanted to become a police cadet, needed to pass four exams in order to pursue a career in the Police force. Unfortunately, he only achieved three. He had chosen to sit one exam without doing any revision and as a result, only gained a 'B' grade which resulted in the option of police cadet training being closed to him.

2. Respect and integrity

This independent action comes when children spill out into the playground. Respect and integrity that have been building up during the early years comes into play. Integrity and respect are moral principles within us and govern our actions and reactions. Our children, by this time, will almost instinctively treat others based on the respect and integrity that they have acquired during the early years under our guidance.

There will be kind children who will become life-long friends, but there will be children who are not so kind and who will want to dominate and manipulate others. Some may bully deliberately and others will bully without realising it but one thing is for sure; we as parents will not be there so our children will have to make decisions about how to handle these situations themselves. They will need help and this is why it is essential that we encourage our children to talk to us. However, we need to be careful not to make the mistake of insisting that they only take a certain course of action, as this will only cause them to keep silent. We can help by discussing the situation in simple terms and looking at the different options open to them. Remember, our children do not have our life experience; they are just beginning to learn about relating to others. We are here to guide our children as they learn to handle different situations.

Here's an example:

> Your child comes home and says, "Johnny pushed me hard today."
>
> "That's not very nice. What did you do?"
>
> "I got very upset and told the teacher."
>
> "That was good. What did she do about it?"
>
> "She just told him that was naughty and not to do it again."
>
> "How was Johnny after that?"
>
> "When the teacher had gone he stuck his tongue out at me and told me I was a telltale."
>
> "Wow, that wasn't very nice. What did you do?"
>
> "I shouted at him and stuck my tongue out at him, and then ran away and played with Jenny."
>
> "Tell me about Jenny; she sounds nice."

It would be wise at this point to steer our child away from Johnny and ask about the new friend, Jenny. Interest has been shown in what our child has experienced, and agreement expressed with how our child has handled the situation. We have also been careful not to lecture or correct anything we might disagree with so that our child will always feel confident to share with us. Discussion can come later if necessary. It must always be our objective to make sure our child is always comfortable enough to share their feelings and thoughts with us and hopefully this will continue right throughout their schooling.

However, bullying can create fear about going to school the next day and it is advisable to bring this up during the evening:

> "How do you feel about seeing Johnny tomorrow?"
>
> "I am a bit worried in case he has another go at me."

"What do you think you will do if he does?"

"I don't know what to do."

"How about trying to ignore him and walking away when he comes near you?"

"But what if he keeps following me?"

"You could maybe tell him that if he will not leave you alone, you will tell the teacher."

"He will just laugh at me and call me names and tell me I'm a telltale."

"Okay, I see that. So how about trying to ignore him without you doing anything to provoke him more – no shouting or sticking your tongue out – and let's see what happens? If he does keep on at you, tell the teacher again, but only as a last resort. If that does not work, tell him that if he doesn't stop you'll ask me to go and see the teacher."

"Okay, I'll tell you what happens tomorrow."

"That's good. Let's see how it goes."

What we hope to achieve with a conversation like that is to get our child involved with how they could deal with the situation. There has also been some indirect correction about the unnecessary behaviour of sticking tongues out and shouting, together with the promise to continue to help the child handle such situations, without lecturing or taking over the situation. This kind of problem-solving is a skill our children need to learn but cannot do alone just yet. By handling it in the way outlined above, life skills are being taught that will help our children later on into adulthood.

As parents, each of us will develop our own way of having these conversations with our children because it will depend on each child's personality and reactions. However, the principles are the same.

Bullying is a major factor in school life and although some children never experience it, others suffer badly. For this reason, it is essential that children are taught to stand up to bullies because bullies thrive on fear and secrecy. My son suffered a bout of bullying when he was in high school but the same principles applied. Fortunately, his relationship with his mum and I was such that he told us about it. The bullying had developed into something quite serious by this time and so we worked out a plan together. The plan involved Martin first taking action, and if that was unsuccessful, I would step in. It was a simple plan that required Martin warning the bullies that he was not going to put up with it anymore – either they stopped or he and I would go to the School Principal, and if that did not stop it, then we would involve the police and bring a charge of assault. It never got past Martin's first warning. After that, there was never any problem with them.

There were three principles involved:

The first was that Martin had to be involved in constructing the plan as well as being comfortable with it, and then being capable of following it through. The second was the independent action by Martin in standing up to them. Thirdly, my promised support if the warning was ignored was a vital back-up for him. It was this that enabled him to give the warning. I had to be willing to make good on my promise to involve the Principal and the police if it had been necessary. If I had not been willing to follow up on my promise, my son would never have trusted my help again.

One of the problems with bullying is that it is often shrouded in secrecy. Bullies often tell their victims, "You tell and you're for it." The reason is that they fear exposure, so the one weapon a bullied person has is to expose the bullies' actions to those in authority. The problem is that it takes courage to expose them. My son felt empowered because he knew I 'had his back' and that I would follow up on my promise. This may not have been the case if I had not shown him when he was younger that I was trustworthy and took his concerns seriously. Otherwise, he would not have taken me into his confidence and I would have had no way of knowing what was happening with him at school. If this had been the case, my son might have felt that he had to handle the situation on his own which would have made school and learning very difficult for him. We need our children to exercise independent action when we are not with them, so they must learn to think things through and, with our help and support, come up with solutions to problems as well as strategies for handling situations that worry them. To achieve this, lines of communication must be kept open.

Chapter 23

Influences

As the years go by and our children get older and friendships grow, there can come a desire to be with the perceived 'in crowd'. This is often led by an outgoing personality who is dominating and often manipulative. They have always been there, even when I was young. I remember there was an initiation process that anyone wanting to join the group, had to go through if they wanted to be accepted into this select group. To be admitted you had to be thrown into a gorse bush. Gorse has very sharp spikes and even to touch it, can hurt. If you got through that, there came dares and these could be anything from hitting some 'lower order' person who was not a part of the 'in-set', stealing or setting fire to the gorse on the local common. Everything was designed to control you and keep you thinking that this put you among the 'top dogs' in the school. Once when I was away on holiday in Lyme Regis with my school, some of the boys had a competition to see who could steal the most books from the local book shop. I didn't want to steal but the desire to be accepted lured me to join in. Of course, we eventually got caught but this didn't matter as much to me as the worry that others would think me weak or cowardly if I didn't join in.

The pull to belong is very strong and it was very important to young people back then as well. Accompanied with this were the unwritten codes; you never spoke of what you did within the group to those outside the group, you never told on anybody within the group, and you never 'snitched' to any authority, even if it meant you taking the blame. This, it was said, was the manly and grown up thing to do – to not comply with this meant you were a wimp and had no backbone. Secrecy covered the whole thing and parents were definitely kept out of the loop. A friend recently told me she used to climb out of the window at night without her parents knowing. It was a group thing; the group had planned it and were waiting for her. Recently the police arrived at a house to tell the parents that their son had been killed in a car accident. As far as they were concerned he was in bed but when they checked, he had put pillows in the bed and had climbed out of the window.

Our children may never be invited or even be tempted to join such a group but we need to be aware of the possibility. How can we combat the peer pressure and secrecy of it? As we think about these possibilities we need to realise how important open lines of communication are with our children and how vital those chats we have with them are as well. Our input may well stop our children getting involved and succumbing to such peer pressure.

There is a statement in the Bible that says; 'Do not be misled: bad company corrupts good character'. (1 Corinthians 15:33)

No matter how much work we put in to try to form good principles in our children, sometimes they are undermined by the particular type of friends they spend time with and the peer pressure they succumb to. The need, then, is to identify the corrupting influences and the non-corrupting friends from an early age. There are pointers that can hint, or even clearly show, that something is amiss. Remember the little girl who happily shared her toys with others until the influence of her cousin and his 'it's mine' character came into her life? It could have been said that this was just her character testing authority as she got older. This, of course, does happen but it is dangerous to assume that this is always the case. This mum was aware because she observed the interplay between the two, and saw her daughter being influenced by the cousin by the sudden change in her behaviour when with him. However, what happens if we are not aware of those outside influences? We are not at school so don't always know who our children's friends are, or what their characters are like and hence, what adverse influences our children are under. We need to be aware of who their friends are from the first days of school and what sort of effect they are having on our children.

We would be advised to invite their friends around to play or have them for tea after school. In that way we get to know them and what sort of personalities they have. When the inevitable birthday parties come around, we can watch to see who dominates and who influences the others for good or bad. Always remember that the hedges are still in place – we are still setting guidelines and providing protection for our children. It is our task to protect them as much as possible from bad influences; where we recognise those influences, we need to combat them and not ignore the dangers we see. When my granddaughter was young there were some friends who were allowed to come to her house, but she was discouraged from going to theirs too often. Why? Because sometimes it is not just the friend that is a bad influence but the parents as well. The parents may have very low expectations of behaviour which are reflected in their own child's behaviour and this can affect our child as well. In this way, any bad influences are managed without too much drama.

All this is quite manageable while our children are young, but as they get older it is more difficult to control the bad influences. It is the established bond and trust built up over the earlier years that influences their behaviour when they reach the early teen years. What we can do when those years arrive is watch for clues that indicate what bad influences are affecting our children's character, and therefore their behaviour.

One clue could be if our children stop telling us about the everyday happenings in their lives because of the possibility of non-approval at home. It is no good confronting them with, "Why have you stopped sharing your day with me?" The result will be a shrug or, "I'm getting too old for that."

Another granddaughter had a friend who had some problems and was in constant trouble. My granddaughter and her friends used to try to keep her out of trouble, but unfortunately, they found themselves affected because they were with her. There was a lot of discussion about the best way to handle the situation (of which my granddaugther was a major contributor), before she herself decided that she would still be friendly to the girl but not get involved anymore.

When another granddaughter changed schools at the age of eleven, she became part of a group that had been close friends from their primary school years. She found the group difficult to break into and one young man was decidedly mean to her – he ended up, among other things, spitting on her, which she found revolting. After talking it through with her mother it was decided that they would make a formal complaint to the dean of her year and after doing this, my granddaughter made sure that she had nothing to do with the young man. This proved very effective because the young man's behaviour gradually became much better towards her. However, a few years later when she was having a birthday party and he was not invited, he asked her why. She told him that her mum would not let him come. His response was, "That's because I spat on you, isn't it?" "Yes, it is." The lad had learnt that there were consequences to what he had done. Protecting her daughter from disrupting influences was mum's major concern.

The thing to note here is that it is very effective when we keep open communication between our children and ourselves. It pays dividends and allows us to share and input into the decisions our children are making. Our children learn that decision-making is a two-way conversation and it is not just parents telling them that they cannot do something. It is helping them make decisions when they face simple or complex problems because we can chat with them about the reasons some things happen – what could have been different or what could have prevented a difficult situation. Of course, there are times when we will feel that a situation requires us to step in and say, 'No', and it is in those times that we need to be firm and do just that.

One danger area is when our now twelve or thirteen-year-olds want to go down to the local mall after school or to the movies with their friends. This is harmless in itself but in those situations, it is not just their friends that are the influence, but others who join them. It is good for teenagers to go out together but that is also the time when major influences outside their group can affect them and when others can seek to lead them astray. It only takes one 'bad apple', or even a sibling of one of the group, to potentially do this. The group mentality kicks in – this is when one of the friends is interested in doing something doubtful but wants the group with them for security. For instance; somebody is smoking or has alcohol and is tempting others in the group to have a go because there is safety in numbers. Group mentality tends toward all trying the cigarette or the drink. How do we combat the possibility of this happening? We could just forbid our teenagers to go out in that way until they are fifteen or sixteen, which in reality is not very reasonable, or we could have confidence in our child's ability to make right choices and resist peer pressure. The reality is that our children have to make their own decisions when they are on the playground or out with friends. We need to have taught them to think things through and weigh up consequences so that when they have to make fast decisions they make them based on good values, character and experiences. They learn these things in safe environments during the early years of their lives.

What we are looking for is to be able to collaborate with them about the situations they find themselves in outside the home, through open, two-way communication. When they are at home they still come under our care and direction. It helps to keep on talking about these situations and discussing solutions with them, but always letting them have a say in the discussion and coming to a solution together. We have to remember not to be so dominating that our children close up and stop talking to us. Remember, it is us as parents that have the task of seeing them safely through to adulthood. We will not do that by locking them in a box until they reach eighteen. As they get older we need to challenge them in their thinking and we need to start this when they first go to school and continue it as long as is possible. If we get it right then the relationship with our children will remain strong right through the teen years. By challenge I mean interjections like, 'Why do you think that's right?' or 'What if you were to look at it this way?' or 'Where do you think that leads?' In this way we are helping to develop our children's ability to think things through and to assess the likely result of any action so that it comes naturally when we are not there.

By the age of five, we should have enough control of our children so that they will have learnt that it is important to obey us. From the age of five, we begin to encourage them to take responsibility for their own actions when away from home and in situations that require independent thought and action. However, we must never abdicate responsibility until they reach the age of eighteen. Even then, if our relationships are sound our children will still be eager to seek our advice in almost everything.

Chapter 24

Peer pressure

In Chapter 23 we introduced the concept of peer pressure. This pressure cannot be underestimated and represents one of the greatest dangers to our children. Peer pressure is the pull of the crowd to conform to the prevailing culture of the surrounding society or a specific group of people. It is not just a specific gang or subgroup, but the prevailing tendencies in society.

Recently I was talking with a person in their late teens who said, "It is great getting drunk." I asked her, "What was so great about getting so intoxicated that you could not remember anything?" "What was so great about being sick and unable to stand or walk properly, or lying down with the whole room starting to spin and you ending up being sick over the side of the bed and having to clean it up the next morning?" To any rational mind when thought about in this way, it is not great, so why did this teenager say that it was? The answer is that she was caught up in the peer pressure of her subgroup of society. It was accepted by the whole group that this was the way things should be and if you stepped out of line and declared that it was not great to get drunk, you would be ridiculed, ostracised and told you had gone soft; and that makes young people feel they are no longer accepted and that they don't belong. It was accepted in that stratum of society that the way you enjoyed yourself was to drink as much alcohol as quickly as possible, regardless of the consequences. This, then, is peer pressure in operation. Nobody has made a law about it; it is just the way it is and it is difficult to break ranks.

When I was a young man I became friends with a man from Liverpool who introduced me to his friends. They were drinkers and came from drinking families; I was from boarding school and had very little experience of alcohol and could not drink the way they did. However, I was accepted into their circle and then trained in their drinking ways until I could keep up with them. One day we got very drunk and all that I described above happened to me. I woke the next morning and felt very sick and remember thinking to myself, *This is ridiculous. Why do I do this? I never want to do this again*! But peer pressure is very strong, and the power of belonging and being accepted is often stronger than common sense, so that morning I walked out into the lounge where some of the others were and said, "What a great party, is there any more drink?" I was caught in the web of peer pressure. I wanted to belong and be accepted and because it was considered a manly thing to get drunk, I reacted in the accepted way. For those young men from Liverpool drinking was something they grew up with. Their fathers were the same; nobody questioned it and everybody accepted that this was the way it was for them. I had been caught in a web that made me feel accepted and that I belonged, and that was very important to me as a human being. This is the power of peer pressure. These emotions are real. The power of rejection, isolation and loneliness if I didn't conform was too strong for me to resist.

Having understood how peer pressure works, imagine our lovely five- year-old going onto a school playground with lots of other new children who come from all sorts of different families and backgrounds. They will all divide into natural groups while making friends. Some will be dominant while others will be submissive, some will be bullies while others will be protective of others, and some will be shy and retiring while others will be solitary and even anxious. They all come from different family backgrounds with different standards and cultural differences.

This is the moment when all of our character training during the early years is tested. We have sought to train our children in the way they should go in areas like respect, honesty, integrity, trustworthiness and loyalty. We have also started to train them in the 'law of consequences'. It is this law that enables them to withstand peer pressure and make sound judgements as to what they will do and who they will get involved with, and, conversely, what and who they will not get involved with.

This 'law of consequences' states that 'for every action, there is a consequence', whether good or bad. The Collins dictionary tells us that a consequence is 'an inference reached by reasoning'. Debating real situations, in a safe environment such as at home, helps us to develop reasoning in our children. Our children won't necessarily understand what all this means (or understand the intricacies of the 'law of consequences') but it will enable them to begin to instinctively react to certain people and situations, and this reasoning will continue to develop by conversation and discussion as we keep the lines of communication open. For this reason, it is important that we do not dominate but seek to guide through debate and reason initially, rather than imposing all our own ideas and values about the situation. However, there may be times when we do need to step in when things are not working out, and only then should we impose our solutions. This becomes more important as our children move into preadolescence. At the ages of five or six we give lots of input into our children but at eleven or twelve we will be looking for the solutions to come more often from them.

It would be unwise to allow control to transfer from us to our children too early. Our responsibility extends right up until they reach eighteen. At the time of writing, my two eldest granddaughters have left home and are at university. They now have to make their own decisions and live with the consequences. We, along with their parents can now only pray that their training stands them in good stead. They are now free to indulge their every whim if they so desire. The judgements they make will largely be based on the development of the understanding of the 'law of consequences' within them. Unfortunately, there are many young people who have not been taught about the 'law of consequences' and end up in deep trouble, as in the case of one young man who ended up drowning in his first days of university because he was so drunk.

There is a difference between childhood and maturity. Childhood is training for adult life. Paul, in Ephesians 4:14, describes childhood as being 'tossed to and fro by the waves and carried about by every wind of doctrine, by human cunning, by craftiness in deceitful schemes'. At this stage of development, during the middle years, our children are in a safe place. If we think about the illustration on page 105 we see that at this age parents are depicted as holding on to their children so they are not tossed about.

We regard somebody as mature when they are able to put the lessons learnt as a young person into practice when they are older and independent. The writer to the Hebrews, in chapter five verses 11-14, describes growing into maturity in terms of milk and solid food. He tells us children need milk because they are unskilled and still developing in stature, while solid food is for the mature, who he describes as 'those who have their powers of discernment trained by constant practice to distinguish good from evil'. This is a powerful description of the outworking of training in the 'law of consequences' and speaks of discernment, which is having or showing good judgement. This comes through training, being shown the right way, and with constant practice.

I practised honesty at boarding school because I discovered that the punishments were much lighter than if I lied. Honesty eventually became so ingrained in me that it became very difficult for me to lie. It didn't mean I never lied; it just became more difficult to do as my conscience gradually became predisposed to telling the truth. Honesty had become part of who I was. I was tempted to lie, but the more I practised honesty the harder it became to do. I remember being asked to help clear out an elderly lady's flat in London. I was clearing out a bookshelf and came across a wad of money; about 600 pounds in total. The immediate temptation was to slip it into my pocket. The temptation was there but I knew how to instantly overcome it – by making it public – so I showed the money to the others who were helping me. In that instant, it was no longer a secret, and no longer a temptation. I turned to the others and simply said, "Look what I have found!" Honesty had won the day.

It is important to understand that in order to make right judgements when faced with peer pressure, our children need to be trained in discernment from their early years. This involves parental guidance and input in training our children 'in the way they should go' in regard to respect, honesty, integrity, trustworthiness and loyalty, together with a generosity of spirit. The hope is that these things will become such a part of their lives that when they are outside the home they will live by these attributes which eventually, as adults, will be ingrained in their consciences. As you talk about real life situations, discuss the pros and cons of them, debate and even argue. This will gradually build up neural pathways in their brains and this will help your children to withstand pressure because they will want to do what is right.

This is what we are trying to develop in our children. Start early; help them practise it right throughout their childhood and it should remain when they reach adulthood. There are unfortunately no guarantees. However, awareness of the 'law of consequences' equips our children with a good understanding of what is going on around them and helps them avoid the traps that can pull them in the wrong direction.

Chapter 25

Parental responsibility

Childhood prepares our children for adult life; ours is the task of helping to prepare and equip them for that adulthood.

In the middle years parents are definitely still in charge and continue to hold responsibility for their children, so we must never become complacent. We see the way and point them in the right direction, checking and correcting them when they go outside the parameters we have set. We should never, ever consider surrendering that responsibility, even when under the extreme pressure of a stubborn child who fights all the way. We may be experiencing this with our child and think, *Is it worth it*? Let me encourage and assure you that it is worth every effort because these stubborn children are often the ones who, in adult life, become leaders, innovators and those willing to take responsibility for others. It is very important that in the development of their characters that self-control is fostered – otherwise, they may become domineering, uncaring people who are only interested in getting their own way. People who want authority must learn to be under authority.

I know three families who all had one child who was compliant, happy and agreeable, and another who argued, screamed, shouted and generally made their parents unhappy.

One couple told me that their child had become vicious and reacted in ways that were hurtful, spiteful and insulting. These parents were determined to hold on and not give in to their child who was fighting them at every turn. They were absolutely determined that their child would conform to what they, as the parents could clearly see, was right. Because these parents did not give way to rudeness and temper, the child in this family has developed into a person, now in her teens, who is not only polite and kind outside the family but also a pleasure within the family. The other two families had no idea how to handle their child and tended to give in. They had no strategies to handle the situations they faced. The temptation was to take the easy road of not provoking their child too much and opting for the 'leave well alone where possible', strategy. They let go too early and in doing so put their child's character development into their child's own hands.

What we should do in such circumstances is very important – hold on and not give in to the pressure of a child seeking to dominate every situation with the objective of gaining control. We should, at all times, try to remain calm, loving, inclusive and respectful. Even in these circumstances, children need the security their parents give. However, no matter how much you might think otherwise, your child wants to have a relationship with you.

It is not wrong for our child to express preferences but to do so in a vicious, rude manner because they cannot get their own way is clearly wrong. What happens to a child who is rude and creates a scene every time they don't get their own way? In my experience they are often bullies and not liked; they create fear and nobody wants to provoke an outburst from them. Rudeness or defiance should never result in a child successfully getting their own way.

This principle needs to be established right through childhood, beginning in the early years and continuing right through the middle years. We should not leave it too late, nipping things in the bud right from the start and not waiting until big problems arise before starting to address them.

I was speaking with a friend who told me she had been a terror in her middle years; always trying to get her own way. She described hours sitting on the bottom of the staircase, stubbornly refusing to obey her parents. The family just used to get on with life while she sat on those stairs. She could never remember getting her own way through her stubborn defiance or rudeness – her parents had not let her go! They held on through the middle years and determined that rudeness, defiance and rebellion would have no reward. As a result, she told me she became a model teenager. She is still a strong woman, has leadership capabilities and is no pushover but she is warm, welcoming, kind and helpful.

There are a couple of important principles that need to underpin the way we exercise our parental responsibility:

1. Every child needs the right to express ideas and preferences. Parents need to be willing to listen and give attention to what their child is

saying, even though it is not always convenient at the time. Consider for a moment that what they wish to say just might be important, maybe not to us but to our child. If we have decided that we are going to be parents who listen to our child, we will find a way to do this, even when it's an inconvenient time for us. We may need to quickly ascertain the content and promise to come back to the subject later if immediate action is not necessary. Our child will know that they are not ignored, even if we end up saying, 'no'. It is the principles of listening and acknowledging that are important, not necessarily the end result.

2. We should genuinely consider what our child is saying. It is easy to listen and then to dismiss without thought. We need to ask ourselves if our child's request or viewpoint has merit. There may be many reasons why it might not have, but to have not listened and considered what they are saying, is to communicate to our child that their views are of no importance. Not genuinely listening to our child can cause them to feel that it is futile to even try and discuss things with us, leading to withdrawal, frustration and anger.

Our children are now more aware of the opportunities open to them and naturally seek to negotiate in getting what they want. This is often influenced by what their friends have or what advertisers push in their direction. Our job is to listen, evaluate and then discuss with our child what they are saying, feeling or wanting. Our role is important because they have not yet developed the capability in themselves of judging the effects or dangers involved. Take electronic gaming for example. Children will sit for hours doing nothing else. As parents we have to ask ourselves what the dangers or long-term effects of gaming can have on our children, discuss it with them and then arrive at an agreeable solution together. Our considerations may be different from other parents, but we must not let that divert us from our own views and standpoint. I know one family who will not have gaming in the house. Their reasons are simple – gaming tends to isolate a child and they want their children to grow up having the ability to relate to others. They want their children to be active and not passive, to read and broaden their minds, and they want the family to interact together. For this family, these things are very important.

You may consider things differently and would not totally bar something like gaming because a family gaming together can be great fun. However, when something like electronic gaming enters our family's life it can be some time before we realise the impact it is having. The problem is that the consequences materialise later on and it then becomes very difficult to remove the cause from family life; accompanied with this can be much anger and frustration from our children.

This is just one of many such areas where we will need to think through the consequences, some of which we will consider later in the chapter discussing electronics. We all have our own ideas and principles and we need to apply them to the whole family and consider the long-term effects they may have. This is all part of the parental responsibility we bring to our family. Talk to other parents and get advice and recommendations to help you consider the consequences before issues arise. Remember that it is important to include your children in the discussions so that they see your view has sound reasoning – they may not agree but they will know that you have their well-being in mind.

Parental responsibility is about training our children to live within our own family and society's code of conduct, and determining the details of what that code is for our family. The key is to think through some of the long-term consequences of behaviours we want in our family culture and to put our family's code of conduct in place very early on in our children's lives. Of course, this needs to be the whole family's code, because we cannot have one rule for the adults and another for the children. We are in this together as a family. If a parent uses bad language then it is unreasonable to expect the children not to. If a parent spends hours in front of the computer, it is unreasonable to expect anything different from the children.

There are, of course, areas where this principle does not apply. If we drink alcohol there are compelling reasons why our children should not! If we stay up late there is obvious evidence that our children's well-being will be hindered if they do the same. There are movies that an adult can watch but a child should not.

Consistency is key. To be inconsistent is to send mixed messages which result in confusion.

So how do we maintain our principles in a consistent manner right through the middle years when defiance and disobedience arise? Here are a few suggestions:

Timeout

The 'time out' concept outlined in the early years will work to a limited extent until the age of six or seven, but will eventually lose its effectiveness. However, I have heard of 'stair time', which is the same idea which has been effective throughout the middle years for some children. Defiance or disobedience results in the child sitting on the stairs for a period of time with nothing to do until the child acknowledges the behaviour and expresses an apology.

Fines

Another idea is a monetary or property fine. If we break the speed limit while driving and are caught, there is a fine to pay. When a child is defiant and disobedient they are fined. This can be material in nature – taking away a favourite toy, computer time, cell phone etc., and if they are still defiant or disobedient something else can be removed. I remember hearing of somebody who emptied their child's room in this way! It can also involve pocket money, which is written in a book a month in advance. When a child commits a misdemeanour they are fined and it is taken from the pocket money total with a note as to why. When the money is due, the child finds the pocket money is less than expected and, more importantly, with an explanation as to why.

Grounding

An example of this is not allowing a child to go to a birthday party, or to see a show or football match. These actions must be thought through as they can sometimes backfire and affect the whole family in an unhelpful way, punishing siblings who have done nothing wrong.

Whatever we do, it has to be effective and consistent, and will almost certainly change as our child grows older. I remember when threatening to withhold our son's pocket money was the only thing that would make our son take notice. He said, "Dad you know how to get me, don't you?" Find the effective action for your child and follow it through.

I am convinced that if parental responsibility is practised early on in a child's life, and is consistently applied, it is much more effective than trying to impose it later when a problem arises.

If you are reading this and you realise that you have handed over responsibility as parents to your children and you need to take back, it is not too late! Fight for your children. Sit them down and tell them the rules and the consequences and what is at risk. It will be hard, but our children are worth fighting for because our goal for them is to develop into mature adults.

Chapter 26

Danger - Frustrated young people!

The objective of the early years was to obtain obedience, but this gradually changes with our children taking responsibility for their own actions as they move through the middle years. The reality is that taking personal responsibility for one's actions has to be learned in an environment that is not hampering or hindering that progress. If we do not gradually release our control but hold on and restrict our children in an unhelpful way, this will lead to frustrated young people.

If children are to graduate into the adult world at eighteen well equipped for adult life, there are certain components that are absolutely essential in their preparation. They are praise, encouragement, understanding, listening, training and discipline. Each of these, which we looked at in Chapter 4, are aspects of love. They need to remain constant right throughout childhood and will release the emerging adult to discover who they are, while in the safe environment of home life. They enable rather than restrict. However, a lack of understanding of discipline will potentially frustrate and kill off any positive effects of the other components mentioned.

By discipline, we mean 'disciplinary correction' – in other words, bringing correction when something is wrong, or when somebody is going the wrong way or doing the wrong thing; i.e. training children in the way they should go. 'Train' means to 'hedge in' or 'straighten up', indicating that children need guidelines that channel them in the right direction. To allow them outside these guidelines is for them to act independently of you when they are clearly not yet equipped to do so. Guidelines keep children from that which harms them physically, psychologically or affects their personality. We are directing them '... in the way they should go ...' There are still times when 'no' comes into play. Parents must not give up their responsibility of care or give independence too early, even if it is the ultimate objective. This is what discipline is about. Discipline is not about punishment but primarily about guidance, with 'no' as an ultimate stop when guidelines are breached.

The injunction given to children by God is that they should be obedient to their parents. Paul, in Colossians 3:20, instructs children to, 'obey your parents in everything, for this pleases the Lord'. However, there is great danger in parents demanding blind obedience at all times, regardless of a developing character that will one day need to make its own decisions. The danger is that we end up with frustrated young people who cannot wait to throw off the shackles created by overbearing parents. Such frustration leads to rebellious behaviour and deceitfulness. The Bible does say that children should obey their parents but the very next verse says, 'Fathers, do not provoke your children, lest they become discouraged'.

The term 'father' in its original language is a root word signifying 'a nourisher, protector and upholder'. To nourish is to provide food and other necessities for growth and health – physical, mental and emotional. Good nourishment provides the atmosphere needed for educational development. A protector is one who makes the environment secure, a sanctuary in which a young person feels safe. An upholder confirms and supports (praising, encouraging, understanding and listening), which makes a person feel that they matter and that their views are important and given due consideration.

It is not difficult to obey somebody who has your best interests at heart and at the same time is releasing you and giving you responsibility where it is appropriate. If we want our children to remain respectful, have an obedient spirit and desire a good relationship with us, their parents, then we need to understand that we can frustrate them by being dominant and overbearing and not praising, encouraging, understanding and listening to them. This can discourage our children which can lead to a loss of confidence and enthusiasm in them and eventually to resentment towards us.

The objective, then, is to gradually release responsibility to our children where it is appropriate. When our daughter was in her teen years, clothes became a problem. She came with constant requests; 'Can I have this; can I have that?' We could not always afford what she wanted, and because she was not paying for the items the cost meant little to her. A friend advised us to give her the responsibility by giving her a clothing allowance. We agreed on a sum we could afford every month and stipulated that the allowance could only be spent on clothes but that we would still pay for all school clothes and underwear. It worked like a charm! Suddenly our daughter was hunting for bargains and making the allowance last in a way which, if we still had the responsibility, would not have occurred to her. We realised that this was also teaching her the value of money; that it is not unlimited and not automatically available but has to come from somewhere.

When our son started secondary school at eleven years of age, I told him that he had to be responsible for his own actions while going to school, at school and on his way home. If he decided to smoke, drink alcohol, dabble in drugs, swear or steal, there was nothing I could do to stop him. He would have to accept the consequences of his actions. I felt that spelling it out for him helped him consider what he was doing so that it would have had to be a deliberate action to deviate from the way we had shown him.

This giving of responsibility can take many forms and we do well as parents to find small things where we can give our children responsibility from a very young age. This will help prepare them for greater responsibility as they get older.

I recently saw a little girl who had been given the responsibility of choosing what she wears when not at school. Let's just say she had a different sense of style and she chose every pattern and colour you could imagine! Her parents had said she could choose what she wore, so she did. It was important not to take the responsibility back by making her change into something her parents thought looked better. My own granddaughter was just like that, and eventually she developed her own sense of style, through trial and error, and maybe a little prompting from her parents, e.g. 'Do you think those things really go together?' causing her to consider what she had chosen. They did not force her to change because they had given her the responsibility and she needed to learn for herself.

In the middle years, we seek to find small things that our children can have responsibility for and we train them by giving them good feedback on how they are doing. Giving them a reward of appreciation from time to time is also appropriate. For example, we can give our child the job of emptying the waste bins in the house. We need to show them how to do it properly, correct them when it is not done or not done very well, but then encourage, commend and reward them when it is done well.

The objective here is to give the child responsibility little by little so that by the time they reach eighteen they are already well skilled in making decisions for themselves.

The reality of the world we live in is that we gain our provisions for life as a reward for the work we do, and we can help our children learn this from an early age. To do this we can link responsibility with reward. The reward can be pocket money or treats, or if you do not like to link the two because there are jobs at home which should be done without reward, a gift or bonus every now and again. We will expand this subject in another chapter.

We need to give our children responsibility for as much as possible as long as there is no danger of them being corrupted or damaged in a way which will materially affect their future lives. For instance, if your child is given responsibility for deciding what they will eat or not eat, you are placing them in very real danger of obesity or ill health in later years. It was interesting watching one of my granddaughters, (who would have eaten all the wrong things continually if given the opportunity) being prevented from doing so by her parents. There was much shouting and arguing but they stood firm. Some would say that this could have caused her to overindulge at other times and it may well have done on occasions, but such opportunities were limited. When she was about fifteen, I remember taking her to a café and allowing her to pick whatever she liked. She chose the biggest cake, but when she sat down to eat this treat (that her eyes had taken a liking to), she could not eat it all and left half of it. Will this always work? Probably not, but surely it is worth the effort to train our children in such areas. The interesting thing about this granddaughter is that she eventually realised that the consequences of overindulging and eating all the wrong things was becoming obese and she did not want that.

Give responsibility where we can, but as parents retain responsibility or partial responsibility for all areas that require further training. If you don't do this, there is a very real danger that you will be walking straight into the trap that Paul spoke about; 'the frustrated young people trap'.

Chapter 27

Tidiness

This is not a straightforward subject to deal with, and I have to confess I don't have much experience in tackling it. My own children were not very tidy and we, like so many other parents, had to fight the battle of getting them to put things away after use and tidying their rooms from time to time. I now watch my children and other parents going through the same thing with their children.

The questions I want to explore are; does tidiness really matter and if so, is there an answer to untidiness with children? As we consider the possibilities you will need to make up your own minds as to how much it matters to you, and then act accordingly.

As a starting point, let's think about what we were like as children and then compare that with how we are now.

My own children, for instance, were very untidy as children but have ended up as adults with tidy homes and are people to whom tidiness matters (one more so than the other). This would tend to indicate that tidiness in childhood does not matter too much in the long run.

I read recently that a child is not interested in tidiness because the part of the brain that governs tidiness is still being developed. This means that they are indifferent as to whether their room is tidy or not and oblivious most of the time to the results of untidiness. It explains why my wife and daughter were not tidy as children, but the question arises as to why they are now tidy as adults.

What factors in childhood helped create (if any) their desire for tidiness and order as adults?

Mary, my wife, is a very tidy person. She told me this could not have come from training in childhood because, although her mother kept the house clean and tidy, Mary was the opposite as a child and very untidy. However, as an adult, Mary has a weekly routine which has become known as her 'Cinderella days' when she cleans the whole house. Where did this come from? Mary's mother cleaned every room once a week and it appears that, without thinking about it, Mary has copied her mother's example – she cleans every room every week.

So, even though our children as teenagers always had untidy rooms, our home was not. Most things had their place and the house was cleaned every week. Our children, as adults now, like their homes neat and tidy. An example had been established, so when my children set up their own homes the principles seemed to have been embedded within them.

As parents, our example seems to be a powerful training tool and potentially sets the standard for our children, but possibly not until adult life[10].

While discussing this question of tidiness with one of my granddaughters, she told me that even though her room is a 'tip', when she has friends around she wants to tidy the house and keep it tidy after they have gone.

So, do we not need to worry about our children keeping their rooms tidy because example could be enough and it will all work out in the end? This may well be true and a possible reason for not worrying unduly about tidiness. However, my observation is that children's untidiness causes continual tension and tantrums in almost every family. In view of this, this chapter is suggesting possible ways to alleviate the tension untidiness generates, and also considers the possible benefits of tidiness for children when the time comes for studying, work and when entertaining.

Let's think about ourselves. How tidy are we?

When people get married they often have different ideas and standards which stem from their own backgrounds and dispositions. When friends of ours got married and were both working full-time, tidiness was not a problem; they both shared the cleaning and tidying the house in the weekends. When their first child arrived mum stayed home while dad continued to work full-time. The new mum did not mind a few toys lying around and washing being left on the sofa, but her husband was a person

---

10 http://www.2knowmyself.com/how_childhood_experiences_affect_adulthood

who liked everything put away and the home neat and tidy. He hated coming home and finding toys on the floor, dishes not done and ironing left around, so he felt compelled to do more cleaning and tidying when he was home. You can imagine the tension this brought to his wife, but the fact is neither of them was right or wrong; they just had different personalities and had come from different backgrounds. Their differences created difficult living conditions and they needed to come to a mutually understood position that did not force one to become like the other.

What are the benefits of keeping a room or a home in a reasonably tidy state?

1. It is much easier to find things if everything has its place and is returned to that place after use. One morning one of my granddaughters was getting ready for school and could not find her school shoes. They were already running late and tension between mum and daughter was high. The girls' rooms were never tidy in those days because they were sharing a small room and this made the situation worse. However, the shoes were found that evening after a thorough search in their proper place! They were not normally put away, so nobody looked there! Orderliness can reduce this common cause of tension.
2. It is harder to put lots of things away at once, instead of putting items away as we finish using them. We all know that if we leave everything out and put nothing away, there comes a time when we are forced to have a big clean-up. It is at this point that it becomes a massive and tiresome chore which inevitably causes tension and unpleasantness.
3. Cleaning a tidy room is a lot easier than trying to clean a room that is very untidy.
4. For a child who may end up studying in their room, it makes for a much more congenial atmosphere in which to do homework.

The following are possible ways in which we can foster tidiness in our children, with the hope that it will affect standards in them as future adults.

Tidiness should be about the whole family keeping the home to a standard of cleanliness and tidiness that is in keeping with the family's lifestyle.

Parents might be responsible for their room and children for theirs, with everybody helping with the communal areas. For each child, this may be a small job like emptying bins, but in this way, you are setting up principles in your family's life.

When children are very young they need some help keeping their possessions in order. However, if it is always done for them, that becomes the norm and this can become difficult to break later. If the family's general principle is that things that are used are put back when finished with, then this ultimately helps to make the task much easier in the long run. If this is practised from the start and everyone is expected to join in, it becomes routine and, hopefully, habit.

Another suggestion made by friends of ours is that the responsibility is given over to our child. They can keep their room in whatever state they like because, after all, it is their room. The only proviso is that every week or so the room will be cleaned and the parents will give the child two days' notice to get it sorted.

Will every child conform without fuss, shouting or slamming doors? I doubt it, but that's not the issue. It comes down to our expectation. If the routine has always been in place, any protest will usually be short-lived.

It is important for us to understand that the underdeveloped part of our child's brain means they may not see the need to be tidy, but that does not mean the point is invalid. So, if you decide (in your family) that tidiness is important at whatever level, you need to establish this with both example and routine. Start at a young age and involve all the family, without expecting your children to understand or like it. Your standards should be clear but allow for some flexibility to prevent tension and rebellion within the family. This is because rigidness and inflexibility only generate fear of failure and are not useful in training for lifelong habit formation. If we set a standard that is rigid and requires all things at all times to be in place, then all we are doing is putting a burden on our children, and this could result in those imposed standards being rejected at the first opportunity. We must be careful never to impose meaningless standards onto our children.

Chapter 28

Sleep

The one thing we know for certain is that children need to sleep. If they get enough sleep they cope with the general ebb and flow of life better, they learn better, they maintain their health better and they relate to others better.

Scientists are constantly discovering more and more about the science of sleep – why we need sleep is not fully understood but the effects of good sleep, or lack of sleep, are increasingly being understood. What we do know is that sleep seems to be associated with restoration, energy conservation, brain processing and memory consolidation. Good sleep enhances our creative abilities and our capacity to problem-solve. Lack of sleep seems to be linked with poor memory, increased impulsiveness and poor judgment. This is, of course, not just true for children but for all of us. The big difference for children is that their brains are still developing and they are learning skills and knowledge at a rapid rate, and good sleep is essential to consolidate all of that development. Not only do they get cranky and irritable if they do not get enough sleep but there is a strong possibility that they may become more susceptible to health problems in later years. There is also evidence that sleep deprivation predisposes us to possible mental illness. Good sleep, on the other hand, promotes well-being[11]. It is our responsibility to make sure our child gets enough sleep because it is vital for their health and educational advancement.

Chapter 5 put forward the case that it was important to set good sleep patterns for our child right from infancy. If this is done the chances are our child will become a good sleeper.

11

http://citeseerx.ist.psu.edu/viewdoc/download?doi=10.1.1.290.4344&rep=rep1&type=pdf

As the middle years progress our child needs slightly less sleep, although it is still a reasonable amount. When our granddaughter was 12 years old she still needed ten hours sleep a night (during term time) but her 16-year-old sister only needed eight to nine hours. Adequate sleep is necessary because our child has a lot to take in during any school day and the less sleep they have, the harder it is to concentrate.

When I worked in the film industry I can remember being so tired during the afternoons that I had great difficulty maintaining my concentration. I did not get enough sleep each night to remain attentive and able to concentrate on the job in hand throughout the whole day. If that was true for me as an adult we can well imagine what it might be like for our child in the classroom.

Rather than thinking about bedtimes, the recommendation is that we think about the amount of time a child needs to sleep in order to maintain concentration throughout the day. The following lists the recommended number of hours a child needs to sleep each day:

3-6 years old: 10-12 hours per 24-hour day

7-12 years old: 10-11 hours per 24-hour day

With social, school, sporting and family activities, bedtimes gradually become later and later; nevertheless, adequate sleep is still a necessary requirement.

12-18 years old: 8-9 hours per 24-hour day

Sleep remains just as vital to the health and well-being of teenagers as when they were younger.

Bedtimes can be calculated, during term time, according to the number of hours of sleep needed. When my youngest granddaughter was eleven she went to bed at 8.30pm and was woken at around 7.00 am, giving her ten and a half hours of sleep. Her sister, at fifteen, went to bed at 10.00pm in term time and was woken at the same time as her sister, giving her nine hours or sleep. We need to be aware of how tired our child is and adjust accordingly – but remember few children like their bedtime put back again, so be cautious in pushing bedtimes out too far until you are sure they can cope with less sleep. Outside of term time, we can be more flexible and even occasionally let our child stay up late.

Not getting enough sleep has consequences and we need to consider and understand those consequences. When we understand this, we can put patterns into place from an early age that help mitigate the problems of sleep deprivation. No matter what age we are, the same applies, so let's review some of the problems caused by lack of sleep:

- Limited ability to learn, listen, concentrate and problem solve.
- Forgetfulness of names, dates, homework.
- Aggressive behaviour such as being impatient and irritable with others.
- Temptation to eat too much unhealthy food, like sweets and fried foods, which can lead to obesity and other health problems.

There is growing evidence that sleep deprivation can contribute to ill health, both now and in later life[12].

Sleep is not wasted time, but vital for the continued well-being of our children. If we want them to flourish socially, educationally, mentally and physically, then the right amount of sleep is vital. It is our responsibility to make sure they get this, and not leave it to them because most children will want to stay up as late as possible.

Insomnia

Some children can suffer from insomnia, the causes of which can be complicated and many. It is not our task here to remedy the many causes of insomnia. However, we do need to understand that there are certain things which can precipitate insomnia in our children.

Lack of a bedtime routine

12

http://www.hsph.harvard.edu/nutritionsource/sleep/

http://www.independent.co.uk/life-style/health-and-families/lack-of-sleep-may-increase-the-risk-obesity-and-diabetes-study-finds-10109111.html

Routines establish sleep patterns in the brain so that they become a habit, and they help set our internal time clocks. This causes us to have a sleep time and an awake time. Most people wake at the same time every morning and feel sleepy at the same time every evening. This setting of the patterns of sleep is disrupted by different bedtimes throughout the week. A lack of bedtime routines such as a bath, reading and cuddles, while our children are very young, may all contribute to sleep problems in the middle years.

Abnormal sleep aids

When a baby is put to sleep at bedtime by being rocked in mum's arms, patted until falling asleep or by a parent lying down with the child until they fall asleep, these are all aids to sleep. The danger is that if we continue to do this for a prolonged period of time, when the child reaches the middle years they will still need some sort of aid to help them go to sleep. This may be music playing or them having to read until they fall asleep. The problem is that this becomes the norm in the brain so that when no aid is there the brain fails to signal that it is sleep time. When the child wakes up in the night the brain feels something is missing and the child cannot get back to sleep until the aid is restored. While such aids are not necessarily wrong, we have to consider the desired end result; that the child needs to be able to sleep when they lie down at night, and when they wake in the night they need to be able to put themselves back to sleep. Their brains need to be trained in good sleep patterns.

Anxiety

There was a time when our son, who was under five at the time, became very anxious when sent to bed and did not like being left to go to sleep on his own. When faced with such things it is sometimes difficult to know what would have caused this change in behaviour and what could be done to remedy it. We did not want to exacerbate his anxiety but at the same time, we did not want to break the bedtime routine we had established, as he was normally a good sleeper. However, we knew that for a period of time he needed the security of knowing we were there. Our solution was to continue with our normal bedtime routine and then leave the room. When he became agitated we returned but sat on his bed without talking, playing or even making eye contact with him until he fell asleep. We only had to do this for a few weeks before our son's anxiety at bedtime lifted and he slept normally again. Even though this happened in his early years, it was important that we completely dealt with his insecurity at that time or else his anxiety may have continued well into his middle years.

School work, exams, friends and family relationships can all bring anxiety. However, if strong sleep patterns have been established in the early years and maintained into the middle years, good sleep patterns will help children better deal with anxiety.

Chapter 29

Work ethic

Work is defined in the Oxford online dictionary as 'activity involving mental or physical activity done in order to achieve a result'. Ethics are the principles that govern how we conduct that activity.

Most of our adult life is made up of responsibilities of one sort or another. How we carry out those responsibilities is vital to our success or failure in life. As adults, our work ethic is very important as it determines how any task, job or career is tackled. Some adults fail again and again because they place no ethical value in the way they tackle a job. Some do the minimum work necessary, while others are always looking to gain a personal advantage. Others have a good work ethic by giving of their best, and always trying to achieve the highest standards they are capable of.

We all have a work ethic and this will show up in the way we conduct ourselves in our day-to-day life. It will be on display and copied by our children. If our work ethic is, 'That will do, I cannot be bothered to finish that', then that attitude will be assimilated into our child's mind, particularly if our child's disposition is inclined that way anyway. This will result in them tackling a piece of homework with that same ethic – 'that will do, I hope it's good enough to pass'. On the other hand, if our work ethic is to do all things with integrity and to the best of our ability, then that is the standard our children will tend to pick up.

We also need to understand that while we want to see our child reach their potential, we cannot expect to see them perform to our adult standard which we, or others, have achieved after many years of training. Children are developing and learning and they do not come with it all in place. Take reading for an example – they initially have to look at every letter that makes up a word until they gradually become so competent that they can recognise a word the instant they look at it. This takes time and practice to accomplish and this will be true in all aspects of their achievements. What they may be able to achieve at five is way below what they will be capable of at eleven. Our child's best cannot be judged by an adult standard – it is their best, not our best. This cannot be emphasised enough. I had a dear friend who developed a severe mental health issue at the age of fourteen, probably brought on by the stress placed on him to achieve insurmountable academic standards as a young child.

Whatever our child is seeking to achieve should be done to the best standard they can possibly reach. If they are academically inclined they will excel in their academic subjects but that same child may find doing more practical tasks very difficult. The reverse is also true.

I know a family where one son is brilliant academically and has a high-powered career in the academic/scientific world, and yet he is very impractical. His brother, on the other hand, is a very practical person who is very skilled in his area of work. Is one wrong and the other right? Is one valid and the other not? Of course not, they are of equal value. I remember telling a brilliant graphic designer I worked with how good he was at his work. He replied, "Yes, but if I was to vanish tomorrow, would anyone miss me?" He then asked, "On the other hand, if the road sweepers vanished, would they be missed?" He was very aware of the importance of the less glamorous jobs, and put a high value on the more practical jobs which make life easier for us all. One child may be capable of going to university but another may be better suited to an apprenticeship in one of the trades. Either way, this does not mean that one is of lesser or higher value – it is simply that they should be encouraged to do, and be, their very best in whatever they choose to do.

Can we train our child to have a good work ethic?

A good work ethic is in the mind – it is an attitude which governs the way we tackle any task, whether it be at school or work. It reveals itself in habits and routines that we help our children develop through demonstration and training, and it comes about step by step, little by little.

One thing is certain; if training for a good work ethic is going to succeed, it has to start right from the earliest possible moment in our child's life. The chapter on tidiness gives us one example of how to start. As we help our child put things away after use, we are demonstrating work, which is defined as 'an activity involving mental or physical activity, done in order to achieve a result'. The work is putting things away and the result is order. If our expectation is a tidy room, then we need to train our child to think that this is the way things should be. As we encourage them step by step, it will hopefully become a habit brought about by our help in demonstration and practical training; no doubt with a good deal of argument along the way as well! For a good work ethic to become a part of our child's character, our training needs to continue right through the middle years.

Every Saturday when I was at boarding school, we had estate duty. This is when all the boarders helped with gardening, weeding, picking up litter and sweeping paths. We all hated estate duty and many would skive off if they got the opportunity, and we always looked for the tasks that were quick and easy to do. One day I was given the task of cutting the hedges. This was a job that was visible to the house rooms and the housemaster's house so I had to be careful to do a reasonable job. I worked hard and managed to get the hedges straight and even. The housemaster must have been pleased with my work because I was given hedge cutting as a permanent estate duty. He was so encouraging that I wanted to a good job every Saturday – and it became a matter of pride. What was being reinforced in me was a good work ethic. I found that I wanted to do my very best because I wanted to please my housemaster who had given me the job, and added to that, it gave me a real sense of pride and achievement in seeing those hedges straight and even. This good work ethic became an important part of me and I believe helped me gain favour with a local film crew who visited the Home to make a documentary about us. I was asked to help them, and they must have been impressed with my standard of work and good work ethic because they offered me a job as a trainee cameraman which led to a career in the film industry.

When I started work my good work ethic paid dividends in that my boss learnt that I could be trusted to do the best possible job. I remember once being asked to produce a special effect for a film sequence which was quite difficult to do. I worked hard on it because I really wanted to succeed with it, and also please my boss who had trusted me with this wonderful opportunity. When he saw what I produced his reaction was, "That's a great piece of work, and I think I should give you a pay rise." The rise was good, but the pleasure I had from his approval and knowing I had done a great job was even better.

Approval, praise, pleasure and words of affirmation are important in developing a good work ethic in our children. The reward is also important because we ultimately all work for a living. However, an inner work ethic is not developed simply by reward. There must also be pride and pleasure in the task itself and the approval of others. I enjoy photography. I enjoy it for myself, but I also love the approval and affirmation of others when they look at my work. The problem with doing a task for reward alone is that it can become our only motive. In this instance our work ethic can become; 'do a good job when it will only be seen by others; the rest of the time, do as little as possible'.

Our world is full of people who volunteer to help others with no reward. Last year my youngest granddaughter set up a collection of non-perishable foods at her school for the City Mission. She then organised a sausage sizzle to raise money for a charity helping children around the world; all for no reward except the satisfaction of helping others.

How we produce such a work ethic in our children is a difficult question to answer. We can see that our expectations and the setting of standards in family life, together with encouragement and gentle correction, approval, praise, pleasure and affirmation in what our child produces or does, is vital. Some say that every task should be linked to the pocket money our child receives and that money should be docked if a job is not well done. The danger here is that completing the task becomes simply an external compliance. Others say that pocket money should be our pleasure to give, and that a bonus for good work every now and again encourages the development of a good work ethic.

There is a family I know who has three daughters who are all very diligent and hardworking and who all study without pressure from their parents. How did this come about? I asked the parents what they did to produce three children with this sort of work ethic. They told me that they did nothing – they didn't push them into studying all the time nor did they set times when homework should be done, and they definitely didn't give rewards for good work or work done by a certain time. The chances that three girls with different personalities and dispositions all ended up with such a good work ethic are, to say the least, unlikely – most parents will testify of the struggle they have of getting one of their children to do any kind of work while another is no trouble at all. However, for this family, the answer lay in the expectations of the parents and their approach to life in general. They are a very open family who set goals and wrote mission statements, and the children were encouraged to follow their individual mission statement from a very early age. As a result, each child developed a strong work ethic and a deep desire to reach their goals. However, their parents admitted that there is a downside to all of this – all three girls tend to over-study and be too driven by results, and consequently become very disappointed if they do not achieve the standard they have set for themselves.

We are not all goal-setters or are families who write personal mission statements, as indeed Mary and I are definitely not. However, we can learn from this family in that it is our expectation of good goals and work, together with our encouragement, approval and real pleasure expressed in the work our children do or produce, that helps to develop a good work ethic. This becomes part of their internal integrity and character, standing them in good stead for the whole of their adult life.

Here are some of the points which help our children develop a good work ethic:

1. As parents, model a good work ethic in attitude and practice.
2. Encourage goal setting for each individual and the family as a whole; this is a good motivational tool.
3. Praise and encouragement generates the desire to improve.
4. Our expectations will motivate.
5. Avoid negative drivers which undermine progress – 'That was good but ...'
6. Be careful of praising the brilliance of a piece of work as this generates the, 'I'm brainy and naturally gifted' mindset. Psychologically this signals that I do not have to try too hard. Rather praise the effort; 'you must have worked hard to achieve that standard of work'. This generates the concept; 'in order to achieve the success, I need to work hard'.

Chapter 30

Electronic devices and the Internet

In chapter 11 'The Electronic World', the challenge was to consider whether long periods of time spent playing on electronic devices prevented social interaction between children and thus stifled social development.

If a child is given a Smartphone during these middle years, it potentially gives them access to everything that is available on the Internet; some of it very good but some of it very dangerous to the young, undiscerning mind. The Internet world bombards us with images that have both the power to educate and corrupt. A friend was telling me about his struggle with pornography. He said that when he was young it was hard to access pornographic material, but today you can access it all in one small device and what's more, you can sit in your own home and get everything without anybody else knowing.

While we know that it is essential for our children to be familiar with the Internet in today's world, we need to be aware of the effect that unfettered access to it can have on a young mind. Thus, we need to know how we are going to handle and monitor access. My son and daughter restricted screen access during their children's middle years in the following ways:

- There is only one computer in the home and it belongs to the family, so everyone has to take turns in using it
- Screen time is restricted
- No mobile phones are provided until they are needed (which was when the children were going an hour each way on the bus to school)
- Phones, iPads, tablets and computers stay out of bedrooms at night
- Phones and other electronic devices are not allowed to be used at meal times

Recently I got my phone out at dinner time and was told off by the grandchildren for having it out at the table! These restrictions have not hampered our grandchildren's use of technology; in fact, they are all (the three eldest are now adults and finished university) very much up to speed with the use of electronics and the Internet but the difference is that they are not obsessed with it. They also read books, interact well with other people and are socially well-balanced. The younger grandchildren are also proficient with the digital world and are also socially capable and engage in other interests just like their cousins. I suggest that this is the desired outcome we want for our children in this digital world.

The opposite scenario is where families allow their children to have phones, computers and tablets from a very young age, and these devices are allowed in bedrooms at night with little restriction regarding screen time. Not only do they have them, but their parents allow full access by providing data. I know of one young man who is almost totally introverted. He spends his whole time with electronics and of those times when he is not, he has large, sound suppressant headphones on. He is very hard to talk to and seems to find social interaction very difficult. I do not know what his parents' attitude was with regard to screens during his childhood. He may have been a very shy boy who found the screen world a safe place, but as a result of all this, he now hides behind the virtual world and finds it difficult to interact with other people.

There are three aspects of the electronic/screen world that can potentially influence and even harm our children and we need to consider these as a potential threat. They are not areas that will be necessarily evident at first through the middle years but they can develop, often without parents realising it. If the adverse effects of the Internet are to be successfully controlled, or if not controlled, minimised, they need to be considered from an early age. If left until the teen years it will probably be too late.

1. DVD's/Movies/internet streaming services

What are we going to allow our child to watch? The age of innocence is not considered very often today. For this reason, even some very young children are watching violent and/or sexually explicit content in movies because older siblings or parents are watching, or perhaps because nobody even considers the content. May I suggest that it is our responsibility as parents to oversee what our children are watching and make sure it is age appropriate? Our daughter and her family were living with us a few years ago, and on Wednesdays, everybody except our youngest granddaughter and I was out, and so it was a movie night for us. When choosing a movie, I would ask her parents, "Is this okay for tonight?" If the movie was unknown, our daughter would look it up on the Internet to check the content. Sometimes the answer was, 'yes', but sometimes it was, 'no'. Her parents were taking responsibility for what she watched. Recently my granddaughter wanted to watch a movie with me and she looked it up herself to see if it was suitable for her age. She decided it was not, so we did not watch it. The older granddaughter wanted to go to the movies with her friends and the same thing happened. The movie was checked on the Internet and, in this case, considered unsuitable. This caused friction but her parents were adamant that it was not appropriate, so she was not allowed to go. It would have been very easy to give in (especially as my granddaughter was angry she would miss out being with her friends) but her parents remained resolute. If you give up the responsibility in the middle years you will never get it back in the teen years.

Another alternative I have heard of was where some parents chose to watch a movie with their child but reserved the right to pause at any time to discuss any issues that arose? I understand that the child didn't like this but again, the parents felt it was important enough to set these boundaries in place. Our objective as parents is to train our child to be a wise and discerning adult.

2. Electronic Gaming

This is something which is very enjoyable, but unfortunately, holds great potential for becoming obsessive. Here are some interesting facts gained from surveys on the Internet:

- An estimated 72% of households play video games
- More than two-thirds of all children aged 2-18 live in a home with a video game system
- A third of all children aged 2-18 have video game players in their bedrooms
- By comparison, half the households have a TV, 29% have a VCR and 16% have a computer in their rooms
- Boys spend substantially more time playing video games than do girls, regardless of age

- The average length of time spent playing video games is 20 hours per week
- On any given day, 44% of boys report playing video games compared to 17% of girls
- Adolescent girls play video games for an average of five hours a week, whereas boys average 13 hours a week
- An estimated 9% of the 3,034 participants in a study showed signs of video game addiction
- Four percent of study participants were categorised as extreme users who play video games 50 hours per week on average[13]

Gaming is the largest entertainment industry for children in the world. Statistics tell us that 97% of children between the ages of 12 and 17 play video games[14]. For some this is harmless fun but for others it becomes obsessive and the habit is, therefore, hard to break. The games are becoming more and more realistic and, I understand, in some cases more and more violent. There is much information on the Internet. For example, teenagers that play the more violent video games for extended periods of time:

- Tend to be more aggressive
- Are more prone to be confrontational with their teachers
- Are more prone engage in fights with their peers
- See a decline in school achievements[15]

Children and adolescents can become overly involved and even obsessed with video games. Spending large amounts of time playing these games can create problems and lead to:

- Poor social skills
- Time away from family, schoolwork and hobbies

---

13 http://www.addictions.com/video-games/alarming-video-game-addiction-statistics/ (2006) https://kaiserfamilyfoundation.files.wordpress.com/2013/04/5959.pdf (2006)

14 http://www.huffingtonpost.com/2008/09/16/survey-97-percent-of-chil_n_126948.html (2006)

15 http://www.addictions.com/video-games/alarming-video-game-addiction-statistics/ (2006) https://kaiserfamilyfoundation.files.wordpress.com/2013/04/5959.pdf (2006)

- Lower grades and less time spent reading
- Exercising less, and becoming overweight; childhood obesity is three times more prevalent in gamers compared to non-gamers[16]
- Aggressive thoughts and behaviours[17]

This may largely apply to teenagers but the patterns are established during the middle years. It is for this reason that we, as parents, should be seeking to understand the consequences of prolonged exposure to electronic video games, especially violent ones.

It should also be pointed out that there are many benefits to gaming which include:

- Better hand-eye coordination
- Better at making decisions
- Enhanced creativity
- Improved language and math skills
- Develops problem-solving, motivation and cognitive skills[18]

We, as parents, need to set guidelines that keep gaming under control. Parents can help their children enjoy these games and avoid problems by:

- Checking the Entertainment Software Rating Board (ESRB) ratings to learn about a game's content
- Selecting appropriate games – both in content and level of development
- Playing video games with their children to experience the game's content
- Setting clear rules about game content and playing time, both in and outside of the home
- Strongly warning children about potential and serious dangers of Internet contacts and relationships while playing games online

---

16 Brain Rules for Baby. John Medina

17 http://www.huffingtonpost.com/2008/09/16/survey-97-percent-of-chil_n_126948.html (2006)

18 https://scholar.google.co.nz/scholar?q=Players+taught+problem+solving,+motivation,+and+cognitive+skills.&hl=en&as_sdt=0&as_vis=1&oi=scholart&sa=X&ved=0ahUKEwiF6eiCx-nKAhUDoJQKHVUpA3cQgQMIGDAA (2006)

- Talking with other parents about their family's video game rules.

3. Pornography

'What; during the middle years?' No, it's not a problem for our very young children, but it could well become an issue at the end of the middle years on the cusp of teen years. The Internet is becoming more and more accessible and our children are learning to access it with ever more skill. It is a startling statistic that, according to one survey, 62% of children's first exposure to sexual material on the Internet was by accident, with only 22% looking for it[19].

It would appear that it is a greater issue for boys than girls. In the survey, almost 50% of young men who took part said that they look for pornography online either all the time (i.e. every day) or quite often (i.e. once a week), but only around 10.5% of young women said the same. Around half of the women who took part (48.6%) never look for pornography online – compared with only 13.3% of young men (4).

A further problem is that young men are increasingly finding that prolonged exposure to pornography is creating serious sexual dysfunction. Aside from pornography, they are finding increasing difficulty in what is termed 'normal sexual relationships with women'. They are practising what one young man termed PMO (porn, masturbate, orgasm), and as a result, find that with real women they cannot get an erection. These young men need to be so mentally stimulated in order to gain an erection and reach orgasm that they are no longer able to relate to women without the stimulus of pornography. Reports also suggest that as a result, women are becoming simply an object, rather than a human being to love. Another more worrying fact is that some women are beginning to accept this as reality.

I remember how startled I was to be consulted by a couple where the husband wanted to watch pornography with his wife and then re-enact it with her. The reason was that he had been accessing pornography long before they were married and needed the stimulation in order to function. She was very disturbed by this. I advised them not to view pornography at

---

19 http://www.dailymail.co.uk/femail/article-2601381/One-four-children-view-porn-12-younger-stumble-explicit-images-ACCIDENT-says-largest-survey-kind-conducted.html#ixzz2z65zrbxe (2006)

all and to develop a loving relationship based on mutual love and care, and this they were eventually able to achieve. But for many women, using pornography is apparently being accepted as it is the only way their partners can function and they would rather have that than nothing at all.

Why am I writing this now? Because the indications are that children as young as ten years are beginning to access pornography on the Internet. Human history indicates that if they are ten years of age now, then they will be even younger as time goes on. With wireless technology and the possession of smartphones, tablets and computers, the possibilities are greater than ever for our children to access material that they are unable to contain mentally, and that may harm them both physically and psychologically.

When I was a young man we had to go into a shop and buy a magazine to see pornography, and even then the content was limited. Hard pornography was much harder to obtain, and we had to go to a club or get hold of what was called a blue film, and that was not always easy to do. Consider how things have changed today. When we give our children a smartphone, computer or tablet, we also give them an open door to everything it is possible to access; both evil and good.

What can we do about it?

The first thing is to understand the possibilities and to take responsibility for our children's exposure to content on the Internet; not just when they are very young but right through the middle years and well into the early teen years. This means not being complacent. We can do this by controlling screen time and making sure that electronic devices are used in family spaces and not hidden away in bedrooms or places where nobody can see what our children are watching. As they begin to explore the Internet we can check the history of what our children are looking at and put blockers on content so that they cannot view certain things; always retaining the right to check what our children have been accessing on the Internet, even on their own devices. Our right to check should be a condition of our children having media access during the middle years, and making this a very open issue leads to very important conversations.

If our children are to avoid problems as adults, and I am convinced this is much more of an issue for men, they need to be aware of the ethical principles that surround this area of life. An example of this are the principles we need to impress on our sons in particular – men do not exploit women to satisfy their sexual desire; women are not objects to be used but are to be loved and cherished.

To achieve an awareness of these principles in our children we will need to work at teaching them respect for the opposite sex and this is largely demonstrated by the way we, as parents, treat each other and members of the opposite sex in general. For example, the way we talk when with the opposite sex, the way we talk when it is all men or all women, the respect and honour we give each other as parents, and our willingness to talk about different types of exploitation including pornography, in day-to-day life. We can talk about these things as the subjects arise, and in this way, we instil in our children respect and, hopefully, a deep hatred of exploitation in any form, and in particular pornography.

If we find our children have accessed sexual material on the Internet, or indeed been shown it by a friend – and be sure this will happen at some time, we must be careful how we react.

Firstly, explain that it is wrong and that we do not approve. Secondly, explain the exploitation involved, and how we do not want them involved in the exploitation of anyone, and lastly, ask them not to do it again. We must then trust them not to do so. Trust is very important but it does not mean that we can't ask them at a later time if they have accessed sexual material or if anyone else has shown them something.

It is important to talk about these things with our children in our everyday lives. When you see something on TV or read articles in the paper that involves sexual pornography, rape or any other form of exploitation, this is the perfect time to discuss it with the whole family. It is in this way that we generate ethical values that help to our children avoid entanglement and enable them to understand the true nature of exploitation and the dangers involved. As part of our children's sexual education, we would be advised to sit down and explain the dangers explicit sexual material can have for their future well-being in sexual relationships. Being aware of the dangers gives us the opportunity of negating the problem and provides our children with a head start which is vital for their adulthood.

When we give our child their first cell phone that is capable of accessing the Internet we need to talk to them about the dangers of porn. One way of doing this is through a book that I recently came across. It is called *Good pictures, Bad pictures* by Kristen A. Jenson and Gail Poyner. It has eight short chapters that are designed to be read by a parent with their child. These chapters deal with the question, 'what is porn and addiction' and describes how the two sides of the brain, the 'feeling and thinking' spheres work together. It explains how porn can trick the brain, and ends with an 'escape plan'. If you have discovered your child has already accessed porn, this site has tools to help you. The book is available from Amazon and you can find out more on https://protectyoungminds.org.

Here are some examples of how some friends handle these issues:

"We are a family of six with children aged 14, 10, 9 and 6. We all use electronic devices for both work/school and play. The range of devices in our house includes TVs, computers/laptops, a tablet, iPads and a game console.

Placing a screen in anyone's hands gives them access to the entire Internet – good and bad. We make use of the protection mechanisms that are available but cannot control everything. Our ultimate goal is to help our children be aware of the potential of computers and the Internet, both positive and negative, so that, in due course, they can make their own informed decisions about what they expose themselves to and expose about themselves online.

We try not to make everything about lists of do's and don'ts but instead find that a few simple good practices go a long way in keeping us and our information safe online.

When thinking about what information any of us shares online we have settled on a couple of guiding principles. (Note that there is no such thing as a 'safe' or truly 'private' online forum or social media.)

- Do not share information that would enable anyone to identify you, or where we live, or where we will or will not be at any point in time
- Never post anything that you would be embarrassed to show your grandmother

When thinking about how we can keep our information safe from people who have no right to it, there are a few simple good practices that help:

- Always protect the login to your device with a passcode or password.

- Never tell anyone your password for anything. If you absolutely have to do so, make sure you change it as soon as you can.
- Use strong passwords. They should be at least ten characters long. If you want to use a password that you can remember, sentences are much easier to remember, and harder to crack than strings of meaningless letters and numbers.
- Never use the same password on multiple sites.
- Use a password manager to help you remember the different passwords you use. There are a number of free password managers available, all of which make it much easier to create strong passwords and to avoid re-using them.

In addition to keeping us and our information safe online, we want our children to learn how to enjoy themselves and spend time in a variety of ways, and not just in front of a screen. Of course, screens come in a variety of shapes and sizes these days. They all count the same as far as we are concerned – TV, computer/laptop, tablet, iPad, etc. We limit the amount of screen time the children are allowed per day. The amount varies between school days, weekends and holidays. Their screen time is also a privilege, not a right. It happens after their homework and chores are done, and not before school, although this eventually becomes unenforceable as the children mature and become responsible enough to have their own phone.

Even with appropriate coaching, our children are not all old enough to understand what they are interacting with, or to make good decisions, or even follow our guidance all the time. Thus, we have a variety of controls to ensure they are not exposed to unsuitable material accidentally and to allow us to see what they are doing.

The Internet connection to the house is filtered using a free service called Open DNS to block unsuitable content. The service allows you to choose a wide variety of different types of content that can be blocked or allowed.

We do not impose any age restrictions on iPad/tablet style devices but we use the built-in parental controls to prevent access to the Internet.

All devices are locked with passcodes or passwords. The children do not know the passcodes/passwords, so they have to come to one of us to unlock the device to use it. This enables us to be aware of what they are doing, when they are using the devices and how much time they are on their devices. If the children are taking their device away for a sleepover, for example, we will remove the passcode for the weekend so they can use it.

Both Microsoft Windows 7 and above and Mac OSX include a set of 'parental control' features that enable us to control when and how long the children can log into the various computers in the house. They also allow us to control the content and websites they can access. The Windows parental controls functionality also emails us a weekly report of their activity.

We have established a tradition that, if the children demonstrate that they are mature enough we will give them a mobile phone at age 13. However, they have to pay for their contract or pre-pay fees.

Personally, we want to delay our children getting social media applications and accounts of any kind for as long as possible. Thus far the only social media access any of our children have is that our oldest has an Instagram account. A condition of having that account is that we know the username and password and either follow their activity or actually have our phone logged in as them – not so that we can post or comment on their behalf but so that we can see what they and their 'friends' are posting and so on.

Our policy with respect to movies and TV programmes is that we actually obey the age ratings applied to them. This takes much of the debate out of whether a particular child is allowed to watch a particular movie or TV show. Having said that, there are two challenges with this:

Sometimes we disagree with the ratings. This can go both ways. Sometimes we think something is rated too high and sometimes we encounter 'PG' rated material which includes some surprising language or themes.

Secondly, other families have very different standards (or none at all) in this area. This has been an issue when our children have gone to sleepovers and birthday parties. The ideal scenario would be that we would clear any movies that we plan to let our children watch with their friends when they are with us, and we would ask other parents what movies they plan to let our children watch when they are visiting with them. This is not always an easy conversation and we haven't always had the courage to have it even when we have remembered that we should.

In all of the above, we are learning and adjusting to both technologies and helping our children develop.

In terms of games consoles or playing games (on whatever kind of device) we again follow age ratings. For instance, if an app is for 12-year-olds, our children can't get it if they are only 11. We have a system where the children ask if they can have a particular game or app. As parents, we then have a look at the app or game and decide whether it is appropriate. Sometimes we use websites like 'Plugged In' to guide our thinking and we are particularly wary of games involving shooting people or anything of a supernatural nature.

The same is also true for books. Browsing the children's and young adult's sections of the library is eye-opening. I steer the children away from any books involving the occult, demons, zombies, vampires etc. or anything where the romantic involvement between characters is overt.

For movies and games, we also use websites such as 'IMDb' and 'Plugged In' to decide whether they are suitable for our children to view.

Chapter 31

Handling money

Can we train our children to handle money wisely, so that when they are adults they know how to budget, live within their means and remain out of debt?

As adults, everything we want to do in any material way revolves around money in some form or another. Money enables us to obtain the fundamental essentials for life; food, clothing and housing. It also provides what is now considered the essentials of contentment or leisure, e.g. phones, computers, cars, and the list could go on and on. The downside of all this is that many of us operate largely with plastic money – credit cards. This enables us to buy without having the actual cash available and this can lead many into debt. Debt is crippling and is created through a lack of ability to control money. This applies to those who have a lot of money as well as to those who do not. The rich are often as crippled as the poor when it comes to debt but on a much bigger scale.

The word 'credit' has a very wide meaning, but a basic understanding of the word would be 'commendation or approval'. For example, a person working on a film production gets a credit in the list at the end of the film. My boss in the film industry worked on the early James Bond film titles and did very well for one of the titles. As a result, the producers gave him a credit alongside the title designer. This was a high commendation. In money terms, a person's credit/worthiness is the amount the banks will allow them to spend without the actual cash being available. The banks judge or assess whether that person is worthy of this credit limit.

All this adds up to one simple reality – that it is essential that we know how to control our money. Without this ability a high percentage of us end up with large debts and some having several credit cards maxed out. I have known people with four or five credit cards all with around $10,000 on each one. In addition, some have a hire purchase contract on a car and a mortgage on their home. I discovered that one family in our church was in perpetual overdraft. When the wages went into the bank they simply paid off the overdraft, and then the family started to go into debt again until the next month's wages paid the overdraft off once more. The bank charges were horrendous and these only added to the problem. As a church, we decided to help them by paying off the overdraft so they would avoid paying the bank charges and to enable them to get back on their feet again. Unfortunately, within six months they were back in exactly the same situation. The problem was they had no idea how to control their money. We did not pay the overdraft off again but instead taught them to control their money by budgeting, and eventually, they paid off the new overdraft and lived without credit.

How can we train our children to handle money well?

Our training needs to be practical rather than theoretical. In other words, they need to learn through practical day-to-day handling of money.

The first thing we need to do is to look at how we handle our money ourselves. There are some real difficulties here because for some parents it is a continual battle juggling money because there is just not enough to go around. Others earn good money but have no budget and money just seems to vanish, while others budget and handle their money well. What matters is the example we are to our children.

This was emphasised to me when I once visited a family to discuss parenting matters. I asked them how they had handled money matters with their children. To my surprise, they were completely open with the children about what they earned and what it was spent on. When the children showed interest, they were shown the budget spreadsheet with the mortgage payment, insurance and so on. They had a white board where they wrote the amount they had for housekeeping that month, and then would deduct any money spent from the total. In this way, the children were learning what it cost to keep the family each month, the relationship between what was earnt and the running costs of the household, as well as the importance of budgeting. All this was done in a completely open and matter-of-fact way, with no agendas to cut out waste or save money. For me, the most interesting and relevant thing was the effect this had on one of the girls, now at university. Evidently, she has a whiteboard on which she writes the amount of money available for keeping her for the week, deducting expenditure as she goes. 'Train up a child in the way he should go, and when he is an adult ...!'

There are three areas where we can actively train our children to handle money well. In the adult world, they only come after we have set aside money for essentials like housekeeping, mortgage, car, insurance etc. Even though our child does not have those concerns, these three areas demonstrate the benefits of handling money well, yet with the freedom to spend as well.

1. The joy of spending

In our family budget, Mary and I each have pocket money; a small amount which we can spend in any way we like. If I want to buy a DVD or have a coffee when I am out, I can do so without taking money from another part of our budget, and without reference to Mary.

2. The ability to save

If I want to be able to have money available for larger purchases or future needs, I ideally need to be able to save up for them. For some, this seems to come quite naturally. One of our granddaughters saves in this way although her sister spends everything! However, it is essential that we all know how to save, as this becomes very important in adult life, regardless of any natural disposition.

3. The ability to give

I mentioned earlier how it was desirable to encourage a generosity of spirit within our children. Without generosity, we become self-absorbed and think only of our own needs, but with generosity, we think of others. To buy a birthday card and present for someone or to give something to a charity is being generous.

We can use our child's pocket money to instil these principles into them. One idea is that we attach spending rules to the money we give them. This requires our children to put an amount away as savings, give them full spending rights over another percentage and the rest is set aside for giving. Giving can be anything which involves somebody else, e.g. birthday presents, cards or charity.

When visiting a friend recently I spoke to her about this. She immediately brought out three pots to show me. Each had a label; 'saving', 'spending' or 'giving'. Her three children each had a set of pots. The ones marked spending were empty while the others had money in them. Every week the children were given three dollars each; they put one dollar into each of their pots. (It was important to their mum that they did it themselves.) Of course, the spending ones went quickly, but the other pots were not allowed to be touched without parental consent. She had opened a bank account for each child and when the savings and giving pots had accumulated sufficient money, they put into their bank accounts. Each child had a bank book and the children were able to record how much money they were saving. They could not spend that money without the permission of their parents so they had to negotiate when they wanted to save for something or buy for somebody else. It would have been a mistake and counterproductive to never let them use this saved amount, but there needed to be a good purpose, need or desire. In this way, they were teaching their children to set goals for themselves and to handle money responsibly.

How long should parents keep control over their child's money?

At least as long as pocket money is given and at the discretion of the children's parents. Obviously, when our children start to earn their own money we have to think again. Pocket money, in the meantime, is a gift from parents and a privilege, not a right, and we need to teach our children to be responsible with it.

Another mum told me that their children had very little pocket money and not enough to use the 'save, spend, and give' concept. She simply asked her children to write down what they had spent their money on. In this way, she was able to teach her children how quickly money went on trivia.

I can remember as a young man, wondering where my money went to, because one minute I had 20 pounds in my pocket and then it was gone with nothing to show for it. The truth was I had spent it on chocolate and the only evidence was the wrappers!

Several years ago, when going through our budget, Mary and I noticed that we were spending a lot of money on coffee and cake each month, so much so that it made us restrict our little treats to weekly outings. Just this simple act of writing down what we spend can be a real eye-opener because we often spend much more than we realise!

My daughter and her husband have recently started to use budgeting software that incorporates the principle of 'pots' for everything – this enables them to control their money more effectively. It has made them realise that they would have paid off their mortgage very quickly if they had discovered this principle some years before! Their youngest daughter uses it to budget her pocket money and, interestingly, she reduced her spending leading up to Christmas one year in order to put more into giving presents for the family. That is how effective an example can be.

As adults, we work to earn money for living expenses, so it is a good idea to allow our children to earn extra money for doing jobs which would not be expected of them in day-to-day home life. The amount paid has to be worth it for them and the same rule applies – some for spending, some for saving and some for giving.

How much pocket money should we give?

I would suggest that there should be a scale that rises with age, with parents deciding what age pocket money begins and what the annual increment is to be. This could be linked to our own increments, e.g. we get a five percent rise and so do our children. There should be an openness about this so our children are given a realistic idea of what is really going on.

When I was a boy on holiday from boarding school, I once asked my father how much he earned. I received a sharp rebuke as it was considered unacceptable for a child to ask such things in those days. The problem I now see with that attitude is that it taught me nothing about the reality of the relationship between what is earned and what is spent.

The objective is to train our children to handle money in such a way that will enable them to be able to control spending as adults, and not plunge into debt the moment they graduate into adult life. All this can be done through our example, discipline and practice.

Helpful budgeting sites:

www.youneedabudget.com/

www.capnz.org

www.sorted.org.nz

Chapter 32

Alcohol and drugs

During childhood, our attitudes towards alcohol and drugs are formed by the environment that surrounds us, and these generally become our norm. This environmental pull has two extremes – from families that have a clear view of the destructive nature of alcohol and drugs, and therefore avoid them and hate both excessive alcohol consumption, smoking and drugs – to those who are born into families where drugs, smoking and alcohol are the norms. It is hard for those born into this latter environment to go against this culture, as it brings confusion, ridicule and often rejection among friends and even within the family.

Sometimes a child will reject an alcohol or drug-fueled lifestyle portrayed by their parents because they see the destructive nature of it in their daily life. However, most children will in all probability follow the example set for them by parents and peers, especially if they don't understand the destructive consequences of this kind of lifestyle. Even though the evidence is there, they do not comprehend how drugs and/or alcohol are destroying lives.

It is in such situations that peer pressure dictates patterns and trends. Jesus spoke about blind guides and that is what peer pressure is like. (1) Jesus went on to say, "If the blind lead the blind, both will fall into a pit." (2) To state the obvious, to be blind is to be unable to see the obstacles or end result. Blindness indicates a lack of knowledge and the Bible states that people are destroyed by it.

Having been brought up in a boarding school where I was given no information regarding alcohol, smoking or drugs, I was very vulnerable as a 16-year-old moving out into society. Smoking came first and this was because everyone around me was doing it and encouraging me to do it as well. It was horrible the first time I tried it, but peer pressure dictated that I should persevere and eventually I was hooked. Alcohol came next after I met a man in a hostel where I was living. We became friends and he took me to his home in Liverpool where he introduced me to his mates who were a hard-drinking bunch. I had no reference points as to what was right or wrong, good or bad; I didn't know how much drink was too much drink, and I didn't know how much drinking was socially acceptable. Even the consequences of drunkenness did not put me off because the alternative would have meant being the odd one out. I never got involved with drugs as I did not mix with anyone who was involved in the drug scene and they were not as readily available as drugs are today.

Today it is very difficult for some emerging adults because they not only have parents who 'binge drink', smoke and use drugs but they have the pressure of their peers expecting them to get drunk all the time because it is 'fun'. Others may not have this pressure but they are vulnerable because they lack the knowledge of the harm alcohol and drugs can do to them. Then there are others who just want to do it because they have been told it is bad for them.

How, then, can we solve this conundrum, as it seems to be a no-win situation? As already stated, our example is good but it is not necessarily enough because peer pressure can be very strong. When your child goes off to university or away from home for the first time, they are often confronted by binge drinking and possibly some who peddle drugs. Even though there are many who don't get involved with this, there are many who will if they get in with the wrong crowd. Peer pressure can be like a science fiction tractor beam that locks on and pulls them in.

How, then, do we help our children understand the consequences and therefore be able to resist unhelpful peer pressure? The best chance for them is when they truly see and understand the consequences for themselves; when they have made up their own mind that they do not want to go down the road of excessive alcohol binging or get into the drug scene. It is too late if left until the teen years to instil this understanding. It has to start way before then, in the middle years.

As parents we need to demonstrate our attitudes towards these things with day-to-day illustrations that teach our children the consequences of excessive alcohol, drugs and smoking. These illustrations feed important information into our children's brains, forming neural pathways which alert and therefore help protect them against things that harm them.

An example you may remember is when a young lady told me how great it was to get drunk. I asked her what she considered great about getting so intoxicated that she did not know what she was doing, and then opening herself up to violence and even possible rape. What was so great about being sick all over herself, sick all over her car or beside her bed, and having to clear it up afterwards? What was so great about waking in the morning with a very sore head? Notice that I posed questions; not dictated or ridiculed. She needed to answer the questions for herself and find her own conclusions. If that sort of demonstrative information is being given in the early and the middle years, it helps reinforce the neural pathways that will hopefully steer our children away from such dangers.

The opposite was true for this young lady. I realised that getting drunk was her part of her culture. It was the expectation of her family and friends, and consequences were never taken into consideration. Getting drunk was the norm and she put up with the rest without question. If she had said she disliked getting drunk it would be going against the group norm and that would make her vulnerable. Just like I did when I met my mate's Liverpool friends; I had to agree that getting as much alcohol as possible inside you in the quickest possible time was the greatest thing and it was what you lived for every weekend. You dared not think of the consequences. The truth was that I had not been trained to consider outcomes.

Our children need to know about the consequences of smoking, alcohol and drug consumption before they are put into a position where they feel pressurized by their peers into doing something that don't want to do. Knowledge gives the power of choice and we need to feed our children this knowledge all throughout their childhood – not in lecturing, digging up reams of information off the Internet, or telling our children not to be like us, but in speaking the truth based on reality. I was able to ask the questions of my young friend because I had experienced those consequences. You may not have had that experience, but there are examples all around us, on our televisions, in our papers, even among our friends. They are visual and graphic but they need to be openly discussed in our everyday conversations with our children. Answer their questions openly and frankly. It is important to allow them to give their opinions and ask questions; it should never be one-sided.

You might consider giving up alcohol as an example, but that would only make it a mystery and mysteries are intriguing. Better to set an example of your own moderate social drinking, and it is better for them to see you enjoying a wine or beer but never getting drunk. Smoking and drugs should never be endorsed but exposed for what they are.

Mary and I have two children. I have never seen either of them drunk even though they both enjoy a drink. They know that I had a hard-drinking period in my life and that I spent ten days in hospital in Liverpool having my stomach pumped because of excess alcohol. There is nothing wrong with having an enjoyable drink, but there is much harm in drinking too much. Our task is to prepare our children for adult life and putting alcohol, smoking or drugs in their right place is a very important part of parenting.

As mentioned earlier, continually lecturing to our children is not helpful. I would suggest that too much direct confrontation tends to make something attractive to try. The saying is, 'They go on about it so much that there must be something they're hiding'. This generates a desire to try, just to see what it's like. The alternative is visual evidence; getting our children to see what has happened to some people who have lived a lifesyle of excessive drinking and drug use, for example. There have been some high-profile celebrities who have died from drug overdoses and others who have ended up in rehab with alcoholism. We can generate important discussion with our children by talking about these things and getting their point of view as well as giving our own. Something that should be a part of the general conversation is how addiction starts, and once it has started how difficult it is to stop. It is better to treat the topic as a general discussion, generated by questions and involving our own experiences. We have an epidemic of drugs and excessive alcohol consumption in our Western society and it is our responsibility to educate and protect our children from this. Through our day-to-day conversations with our children, I am persuaded that we have a better chance of enabling our children to make better choices.

Suggestion: Have a list of questions on all sorts of topics; some serious, others funny and some even stupid. Get the list out at mealtimes and get somebody to pick a question and then discuss this over the meal.

Some of the questions could be:

- Would you rather be ugly or rich?
- Would you rather be poor or beautiful?
- How much alcohol is too much?

- What effect does it have when you ignore somebody?
- What are the long-term effects of taking drugs?

You could have questions on many subjects; only remember they should not be statements but questions that stimulate discussion. Everyone should be allowed to talk and not be interrupted until they have finished talking. This is a great opportunity to share with our children some personal experiences and some consequences of our actions as well.

1. Matthew 15:14
2. Luke 6:39 and Hosea 4:6

Chapter 33

Boy/Girl awareness

I was speaking to a mum recently who was sharing with me an account of her ten-year-old son's attitude to girls. It was very simple; 'Yuck, who wants to know about girls?' I recently heard of some boys who said, "Have a girlfriend, get married? No thank you." I remember my own children going through this phase at around nine or ten years of age. However, I also remember the growing awareness of the opposite sex and the beginning of attraction. This may occur right at the end of the middle years or in the teen years, but as sure as night follows day it will happen. When it happens it is largely too late to input standards into the situation, even though, as we see from nine and ten-year-olds, there is a phase where they do not want to hear about relationships with the opposite sex, let alone consider the implications and protocols that go with such relationships.

I am thinking not so much about sex because, as parents, we are very aware of the need for sex education, and this happens in school whether it is in a manner we may or may not prefer. I am thinking about what attitudes and predispositions we may hold and wish to pass on to our children. The question arises as to how we want our children to conduct themselves when attraction to the opposite sex starts to occur. If we are to influence our children's attitudes, then I believe we must do so in the middle years.

We live in a world which seems to suggest to young people that there are no moral principles on which to base their actions. If we do not act to influence our children then the general public's attitudes will prevail, and we may not like the result.

While I was spending time with my hard-drinking friends in Liverpool, I noticed that when it came to girls, they had different principles. The first principle was to go as far as they possibly could with a girl, and they did.

However, if a girl objected to their overt sexual advances, another principle came into play. The guys will hold great respect for her, so much so that they looked at her in a different light, and she became someone that they would consider as a potential wife. This was not verbalised, but to an outsider like me, it became very obvious – the male of our species has always had this drive to conquer but when resisted by the female of our species she becomes more attractive.

Contrast my Liverpool friends' attitude with the experience of a young relative of mine who told me that in her circle of friends, if a boy asked her out it was expected that she allow him to have sex almost immediately. She dared not refuse because she would be labelled frigid and this would be plastered all over social media – something to be avoided at all cost – so it was better to give in.

When we are attracted to somebody, then fall in love, we want to spend the rest of our lives with them. The old fashioned term, 'courtship', explains that concept and properly understood, it reveals much. To court somebody is to attempt to win them over with a view to marrying them. Attraction leads to courtship and courtship leads to marriage. Today we use such phrases as, 'like', 'have a crush on' or even, 'have a thing for', or 'fancy'. The basic idea seems to mean anything from, 'I like the look of him', to 'I fancy having sex with him'. It does not seem to carry the concept of courtship, which is 'I am pursuing you because I think I would like to spend the rest of my life with you'.

I remember a man who had fallen so much in love with a particular girl that he would drive between four to five hours each way every weekend to be with her. He said he just could not stand not seeing her. Another man met a girl who was not interested because she had her life mapped out and marriage was not in the plan. He could do nothing to persuade her so he set himself to pray and fast until she realised that marriage to him was exactly God's plan for her. Neither of these men were after sex or even just a girlfriend – they wanted to spend the rest of their lives with these women.

Our objective is to train our children for adulthood. Who they marry is arguably the single most important choice they will make. Marrying the wrong person could lead to a miserable life and to heartache, and possibly divorce. The mistake is to think the relationship is all about sex when in reality the questions that are important are:

- Do we enjoy just being together?
- Can we laugh together?
- Do we have complementary interests?
- Can we be silent and yet be content together?
- Do I hate being apart from him or her?
- Do I just think he or she is the greatest person?

If answers to these questions are positive, there comes an increasing desire for a couple to spend the rest of their lives together.

Being single is a time for adventure and enjoyment whilst young and free. For this reason, some parents I know have established ground rules in the middle years before their children are attracted to the opposite sex. These ground rules need to be planted into our child's mind before the reality of that attraction kicks in.

These are some of those ground rules I have seen in families I know:

Firstly, no boyfriends or girlfriends while attending school. This is not only for the reasons above but because romantic attachments deflect concentration from academic studies like nothing else. Exclusive boyfriend/girlfriend relationships tend to become introverted and cut young people off from life around them.

Secondly, their children are encouraged to remain part of a group of friends rather than singling out one person. A young person may be attracted to another individual within the group but it is better to wait and be a part of the group until school days are past.

There are two questions we need to ask ourselves:

1. The first is; what principles with regard to sexual attraction, courtship and marriage, would we as parents like to instil into our children?

Here are some of my thoughts to help clarify our minds. If the Bible is our guide then we will believe that sex is for marriage between a male and female. The period leading up to marriage is preparation time, or, in today's language, dating. This allows the couple to get to know one another and prove the validity of the initial attraction. This leads to a proposal and if the answer is 'yes', to engagement; this is where the couple commit to spending the rest of their lives together. They would not live together or have sex until marriage.

You may not take a Biblical viewpoint and may be happy with the trends of today's society where sex outside of marriage is acceptable. Many move in together, some never marry and others get married later on in life.

Mere attraction can be deceiving because it is not this that counts in the long run, but it is rather the blending of compatible personalities that makes for a sound marriage relationship and partnership. Many people today believe it is all about sex, but in reality, sex is a small but very enjoyable and necessary part of married life. The majority of married life is about compatibility and enjoyment of companionship, which enables us to face the ups and downs of living in our world together.

The point here is not the rights or wrongs of what we believe, but whether we know what we believe and are happy to pass those values on to our children. Are we happy for them to follow our example? If we are unhappy for them to follow us, we must ask ourselves the reason why. What have been the consequences of our actions that we would like to be different for them? This should be settled between us as parents; otherwise, confusion will be the result. Even if we, with hindsight, would change the way we conducted ourselves, it is not too late to input something different into our children. We will need to talk about what we would do differently and why during general conversations over time; not in lecture form, but by gradually passing on our ideas and information that will form patterns in our children's brains, i.e. the gradual forming of concepts based on good practice and demonstration. For example, 'We did (this) but the result was (this) and we now would rather have done (this), and this is why'.

We must always remember that if we do nothing we simply open our children up to the standards of the world around them and this may or may not be fine with us.

However, an example is only part of the equation. Our children accept our marriage as the norm. They were born as part of our shared lives and just accept the status quo because they don't know any different. If there are standards, they are accepted as the norm but not necessarily understood. If our children are to understand our standards these need to be verbalised over the whole of their childhood, so that they understand the principles behind our marriage, and therefore, their family life.

2. This brings us to our second question – How can we instil principles into our children before they become interested in the opposite sex?

There are many people who think that we should just let our children make up their own minds when they become adults. The problem is that for them to make good decisions they need to be aware of all the facts. There are, frankly, too many traps they can fall into if they don't have enough information or any guidance concerning appropriate standards of behaviour. It is our responsibility, (to the best of our ability), to pass on sound principles to our children. If, when they become adults, they wish to go another way, then that is up to them and we must let them go, knowing that we have done our best to give them good information and guidance.

Our brains pick up repeated information through sight, discussion, teaching, and positive and negative outcomes. This forms neural pathways or habits within the brain. The more we repeat something and use that portion of the brain in a focused way, the more neural pathways develop. Children's brains slowly develop the neural pathways that determine future attitudes and habits. I have heard it likened to a string that, with use and influence, becomes a steel rope and therefore difficult to break.

We can now see why it is important to know and drip-feed what it is we want to pass on to our children, and not leave it to random choice which involves many pitfalls. We drip-feed these principles throughout childhood, and in doing so, help develop our children's neural pathways. This, of course, means they can be developing both negative and positive pathways. If domestic violence or verbal abuse is normal in a child's family, a generational pathway is formed that is difficult to break.

Mary and I have a deep-seated belief that the best pathway for happiness, security and long-lasting relationship lies with the Biblical model; attraction, dating or developing relationships, proposal, engagement and marriage. Is it any surprise, then, that this is the path our children chose and that our, as yet unmarried, grandchildren have declared they intend to follow? The result for us has been seeing our children in stable relationships, even though we know that it has not always been plain sailing for them. We are also seeing our grandchildren grow into adults of good character, even though they have had all the ups and downs of childhood and teen years.

- What then do you want to pass on to your children?
- Are you talking about it, discussing the concepts and results?

If you are not, then are you happy for your children to go with the flow of this world's ways?

Chapter 34

Expectations at the end of the middle years

We have come to the end of the middle years and are about to enter the teen years. Thirteen is, of course, the official start, but it depends on each child. Some, at 13, are not pushing for independence but are quite content to remain quiet and are fairly undemanding. Others are definitely pushing for more independence and autonomy over their own lives.

As parents we have been trying to be consistent in our input, and consistent in our love and acceptance of our child. Through all of this we have been seeking to create in them a sense of belonging – that feeling of being a loved individual within the family. We have been seeking to develop their personality, to influence their attitudes about friends and to combat the peer pressure that comes through media, friends and school. There is no way of categorising all children, for all have different personalities and dispositions – some are shy while others are extrovert; some are practical and others academic.

The early and middle years have blended into one, and the teen years will be added to the whole; making one childhood. That childhood remains the foundation of their lives even when they are old. My own childhood is very much a part of who I am today. It may not have been pleasant but it is still there in me, still influencing me. The way we are as adults is a reflection of our childhoods.

Having come to the beginning of the teen years and the start of the final road to independence, what in general terms do we hope to see as our child is about to enter the teen years? This isn't easy to answer because there are so many variables involved. However, there are some characteristics that are good to see. I have observed these in our own children and in our five grandchildren. These characteristics, I have to say, have been consistent in them all, regardless of personality, and have continued to develop through the teen years and into adulthood.

Just in case I give the wrong impression, I would like to say these character traits listed below are generally true. The reality is that there will always be outbursts, shouting and the announcement that it is, 'just not fair!' If this was not the case to one degree or another, then I would be concerned, because this is normal in every family situation I have observed. Our teenager's brain is still developing a sense of responsibility and this will not be complete until they are in their early 20's.

There are four simple things to help us gain some reassurance that we are on the right track. These are not exhaustive but give us a general indication.

1. Involved in family life

Our child is a part of family life rather than separate from it. It is not an uphill battle to get them to join in and they do not feel as if they are separate from us or their siblings. They are helpful, take part in family conversations and debates and are willing to both listen and express their own opinions, even though we sometimes feel they think they know it all! They are happy to sit with the family at mealtimes and don't always want to eat and run. In general, they love to be with the family and join in whenever there are games and fun happening.

2. Polite and interested

Our child is polite and welcoming to visitors and strangers at home. I have visited many homes where children do not talk to visitors. They will not even look at them and vanish into their own rooms as soon as visitors arrive and are never seen when they leave. On the other hand, I have been to homes where children are welcoming, polite, interested in what is happening and want to hang around during the visit. They are interested in the conversation and express their own opinions if they wish to. In my mind this is partly to do with temperament and partly to do with upbringing. I have observed the very shy still being welcoming, because they have not only been taught but have also been required to be polite and welcoming, until this has become part of who they are within the family.

3. Good reputation

Our child has a good reputation outside the home. When parents are told in a school assessment that their child is polite and helpful, parents can sometimes react with, 'Are you talking about my child? Are you sure you have got the right name?' Their child has those explosive moments at home that they don't seem to have outside the home. This is a very good sign and shows we are on the right track, because the place they should be having outbursts is at home and not outside of it! At home their character is still being developed and it is the one place where they should feel very safe and therefore can fly off the handle with no warning. Do not worry! It is far better to have this going on at home than outside of it. Many times I reassure parents that their children are doing okay - and yes, it is a job to hold on sometimes. But if the outbursts are going on outside the home it means that the regime at home is possibly too strict and our child has no outlet to let off steam. If our child is perfect at home but creating problems outside the home, there is also a possibility that they are involved in bullying or unsocial behaviour.

4. Generosity

Our child has a generosity about them towards those who are struggling and in need. This is difficult to define because it depends a lot on our child's personality type. For some it is natural but for others generosity does not occur to them and has to be learnt. Nevertheless, all of us need to be givers as well as receivers; it is one of the marks of a well-rounded personality.

Our task has been to develop the character of our child and is largely completed by the end of the middle years.

Even though the four-character attributes above are there at the start of the teen years, there are many ways during the teen years that these characteristics can be affected and their growth knocked off course. As parents you still need to be on your guard, providing the security our teenagers need to be able to withstand the influences that will be pushing, through peer pressure, to influence them.

In the final section titled, 'The Teenager' our child's march towards independence and adulthood continues.

Part Three

The Teenager

Caution

I would suggest that the time to read Part three 'The Teenager' is when your child reaches around ten years old. Much of how you parent is achieved during the early and middle years, however there are some significant changes necessary during the teen years.

Introduction

The Teenager

The word 'teenager' conjures up a picture that is created by experience – firstly, by the experience of our own teenage years, and secondly by the visual portrayal of teenagers in the media or on television. This is where we generally only see the outrageous – binge drinking, teenagers out on the town and throwing up after a night of too much alcohol or killing themselves while driving fast after refusing to stop for the police.

This visual portrait of teenage life may have given you the impression that this is normal for the teenage years. For this reason, you may be filled with dread as to what these years will bring both for you and your children. Mary and I see this portrayal of teen life in the public arena, yet our actual experience is very different. Our two children did not rebel, binge-drink, try drugs or stay out late partying, nor did we ever see such behaviour in our five granddaughters. We also know many other teenagers who have not indulged in the portrayal we see in our media. However, we have seen shouting, tantrums, sulkiness and the declared 'It's just not fair' syndrome.

When friends of mine heard of my intentions to write this book they expressed concern that I would express the view that everything with regard to teenagers is sanitised and straightforward and that if you do certain things, then there will be no problems. Their experience was very different because their lovely son became a nightmare during his teen years, and another friend's children ended up serving prison sentences. However, the fact is that the majority of teenagers I have known have been great, responsive, polite and hardworking even though they have also exhibited all the usual teenage tendencies.

The truth is that there are no guarantees, and yet for our children's sake we must never give up. To a certain extent, the way we handle these years will help to guide and protect our children as they go through the teen years and develop into adults.

There is no doubt in my mind that the way we handled the early years and reinforced and developed with consistency our parenting skills during the middle years has a direct bearing on how our children react during the teen years – not guaranteed but certainly a strong influence on the majority of teenagers. My hope is that as you explore these chapters it will help you not only understand the teen years but also celebrate them. To celebrate because there are some great young people out there who we can help to be great adults.

Our youngest granddaughter is now sixteen years old, bright, and often finishes her work at school early. There is a lad in her class who is having difficulty with his work and so she has started helping him. She began to reassure him that he could do the work where everyone else had more or less written him off. He is now achieving much better grades and the teachers have acknowledged that this has only happened because of her efforts with him. Not only does she do this but she also arranges canned food collections, both at school and at our church to help feed the poor and puts on bbqs at school, church and outside the DIY store to raise money for the City Mission.

That we can celebrate, and there are many other teenagers who do similar things.

As parents, you are crucial during these final years of adolescence. They need you and it is important that you believe this; never allow anyone to tell you otherwise. Your job is not done; the way you do it may need to change but you are vital during this last push to adulthood.

Teenagers cannot be lumped into one mould nor can you guarantee how they will react to the growing awareness of the adult which is trying emerge. It is a bit like the butterfly trying to struggle out of the chrysalis – it cannot get out without a struggle and even when it does emerge, the butterfly has to stay still while it dries out and settles into this new form. Only then can it take off into the new bright world into which it has emerged.

Young people are transitioning into a new world; the world where they have to eventually provide for themselves, make their own paths, and explore this world without anybody directing them. The 'hedges' parents have put in place will eventually go, but hopefully, will not be forgotten. Our task is to make this transition as easy as possible and not cramp this emerging adult in an unhelpful way. To cramp somebody is to inhibit their development. The dictionary defines cramping as 'to hinder, impede, constraint, obstruct, block, check, retard or handicap'. When put like that, most of us will realise that that is not what we want to do – rather we want to help, facilitate, encourage and guide. We must release and yet still be responsible, we must encourage and yet still provide help, and we must love while being willing to take risks. Above all, the realisation is that we are still parents and ultimately responsible until our teenager reaches adulthood.

Chapter 35

The past is the indicator of the future

The general disposition of your child probably will have always been loud or quiet, introvert or extrovert, practical or academic, or a combination of these and other personality traits.

Within that disposition their character has been developing throughout their early and middle years. Character is defined as 'the combination of those traits and qualities distinguishing the individual nature of a person'. These traits and qualities combine to make up a person's reputation and are seen in the attributes they display in everyday life. For example, honesty, kindness, integrity, respect for others, helpfulness, generosity and self-control. These are all characteristics of a good reputation. A bad reputation may present itself as jealousy, anger, envy or selfishness. This reputation is visible to you as family, those outside the family and at school.

By the time the teen years arrive the general character of your child is mainly established. Their character has been forged through your training and example from birth and is displayed within their personality's innate disposition.

The development of character was the goal of the early years and the consolidation of that character has been the task of the middle years. Your training has formed neural pathways in the brain that have been established through consistency, repetition, instruction, example and environment until they have become established behaviours. For example, if you have worked hard at establishing honesty and your child has displayed honest tendencies, they are unlikely to suddenly become dishonest when they reach teen years. What about respect? You have worked hard at getting them to say 'please' and 'thank you', and you have insisted that your children do not ignore people but respond and talk to visitors so are they unlikely to now ignore people and be rude and forget their manners? If your child has been taught to be helpful, then they are unlikely to turn into a monster who never lifts a finger to help?

As always, this is the general rule as neural pathways, once established, are difficult to break.

The question is not what will happen in the teen years, but what has happened in the early and middle years? Because it was then that the battle for character was won or lost. It is not that the teen years are easy, or that there will be no problems – quite the contrary. In the next chapter, we look at what is happening in the teen years and discuss how the nature of this stage of life brings its own set of difficulties. However, it is important to note that the best indication of the future is still the past.

As you look at the character of your child until this point in time, you will see a picture of the future. You may lose sight of that picture if things get difficult during the teen years, but for the majority of our teenagers that statement will hold true. Even if there is a divergence away from this norm for a while, that character will generally resurface as true maturity is reached. A worker in youth health told me that those brought up with good principles and who then move away from them in the teen years, usually return to those principles as they reached adulthood.

I have now watched seven children, close to Mary and myself, go through the teen years and come out the other end, with the character development that we saw throughout childhood holding up well. All seven had different personalities but had been given consistently good training and example in developing their characters.

Please do not take this to mean that all was perfect; there were lots of times when they pushed the boundaries, and generally behaved in an immature teenager way. However, through all of this, their characters held true and their reputation at school, in the wider family, church and with friends, did not change. The helpful one who would do anything for anyone continued to do so. The one who was very private and did not like personal things expressed in public was still like that. The one who always spent every cent they had, still did so, the saver still saved and the one who gave to others more than was necessary still did so. They were still polite to strangers, joined in conversations, were helpful to those in need and generally generous. However, that did not mean they were angels at home. On the contrary, teenagers are often difficult at home while being helpful and considerate when away from the home environment.

Does that all just sound too good to be true? When looking at the detail it probably does, and by detail I mean when you are going through tantrums, having to put up with yelling, doors slamming, sulkiness at home and hurtful comments, it can seem overwhelming. But zoom out and look at the bigger picture. What is happening at school? How is your teenager outside the home? When I look at our seven young people, we see seven teenagers who were consistent with how they were in the middle years but who were also pushing for the freedom to live as they wanted to; in other words, they were looking for self-determination. The main focus of that pushing was in the home environment because that was where parental authority lay. In a teenager's eyes parents do not always understand that they have gone past the child stage and are now well into the emerging adult stage. Teenagers always feel that they are quite capable of deciding life's issues for themselves.

When looking at the future of our children it is important to look at where they have come from, and from that, you have a very good picture of where they will end up as far as character is concerned.

However, be warned! – I have painted a picture of an outcome based on consistent inputting of values and discipline, not only through teaching but example as well – initially, in the very important early years where character and parental authority are established, and then in the middle years when that work was continued with consistency in consolidating the work begun in those early years.

The message is clear – one of the most powerful tools for bringing up our children is the example of our own lives as parents. To paint the extreme picture – if you are gang associated, violent toward others, steal, cheat, lie, swear, and drugs and drunkenness are the norms in your family, do not be surprised when your teenagers go in the same direction. When they are children you can forbid them to swear, but as the old saying goes, you must 'practice what you preach' as was the case of a man I came across who swore prolifically. He would give his son a hard clip around the ear if he was caught swearing and threatened him with much worse if he heard him swear again. The motive was clear – he did not want his son to be like him, but the reality was that his son was exactly that. The son just avoided swearing in front of his father as much as possible because of his father's reaction. One of my mates came from part of a community where all the fathers spent hours in the pub after work and drunkenness was the norm. Guess what? All the sons followed the same way! On the other hand, families in high-paying professions may not swear and get drunk but neither do they necessarily correct or train their children in good character. Work and money come first but the result can be just the same – teenagers rebel, get drunk and try drugs because there has been no consistent example set in the years leading up to the teen years.

If your values are consistent and the hedges that you set up in the early and middle years stay firmly in place, then your children have every chance of negotiating the teen years and come into adulthood in good shape. During the teen years parents still need some hedges in place which block inappropriate behaviour and challenge inappropriate concepts but those hedges will have a greater freedom built in them. However, we must remember, that we as parents are still the ones who bring security, safety and provision to our teenagers even when they are craving independence. They are not quite mature enough to handle it, even if they think they are!

Chapter 36

The teenage brain

If we are to understand what is happening to our child now they have reached adolescence, we need to try to comprehend what is happening in their brains.

The prefrontal cortex of the teenage brain is not yet fully connected. Let me give an example – Mary and I live in a private lane and on the front of our property is a street light that has not been working in the six years we have been living there. We decided, with our neighbours, that we wanted this and another light working. We decided to connect them using an extension lead plugged into a socket in our garage. We tried it as a concept test and it worked fine, but there was a problem. How could we somehow program it to know when to come on? Our street light needed a 'sunset switch' which sensed when it was nearly dark so the street light knew to switch the light on.

Now, that is similar to our teenager's brain. It's plugged in and working but has not yet fully developed the means of evaluating choices, making decisions and acting accordingly in some situations. Why? Because there is a part of the brain that is still not fully connected up.

Our teenagers do not have their prefrontal cortex fully connected and this inhibits their ability to fully reason things through and often manifests in risky behaviours. The prefrontal cortex is the section of the brain which enables us to make decisions and plans, weigh outcomes and form judgements, and control impulses and emotions.

When we understand the implications of this lack of connection in the prefrontal cortex of our teenagers, their behaviour and lack of sound judgement in decision-making begins to make sense. They are not just being difficult or rebellious just for the sake of it. Even though they think they are quite capable of taking charge of their lives, the fact is that they cannot fully do so. This makes them prone to taking more risks. Because the prefrontal cortex is not fully connected, teenagers make decisions based on what they feel; in other words, they give an emotional response, rather than a thought-out one that relies on facts or evidence. It may be abundantly obvious to us, but they just do not see it that way, nor do they seem to consider the possible effect on other people or the dangers that are involved.

It would seem then that our first response should be to address the emotional issue. This can be as simple as saying to our teenager, "I can see that this is hurting you ..." or "I can see how painful this is to you ..." The emotion needs to be addressed before we can come in with any parental authority.

Have you ever wondered why teenagers so often seem to lack judgement, especially when they are with their friend's – judgement that on occasions could save their lives? We see it on the news where a bunch of teenagers have stolen a car and then crashed it after a high-speed chase with police. Their prefrontal cortex is not fully connected and as a result the teenagers have responded out of emotion rather than reason and sound judgement, often with tragic outcomes. However, we need to put this statement into context as the teenagers who do this are in the minority and most will never get into this kind of difficulty.

I remember a relative in my own family who was usually a sensible teenage lad; he was polite and courteous and never in much trouble. One day his mum was summoned to his school because he had been caught kicking and pulling fences down in the village and generally making a real nuisance of himself. The family could not understand it, as it was completely out of character. However, they did understand when they realised that he had been with a group of friends and one or two started the prank and the others got drawn in. Afterwards, he was very contrite and realised that he had hurt other people.

Another teenager was killed because he rode his bike in the early hours with no helmet, no Hi-Vis jacket and only a headlight. He had been warned of the danger but he just could not see it; to him it was fine until it was too late.

As parents of teenagers, it is important that we understand these facts because it powerfully affects what we do as parents. Have a look again at our illustration of hedges.

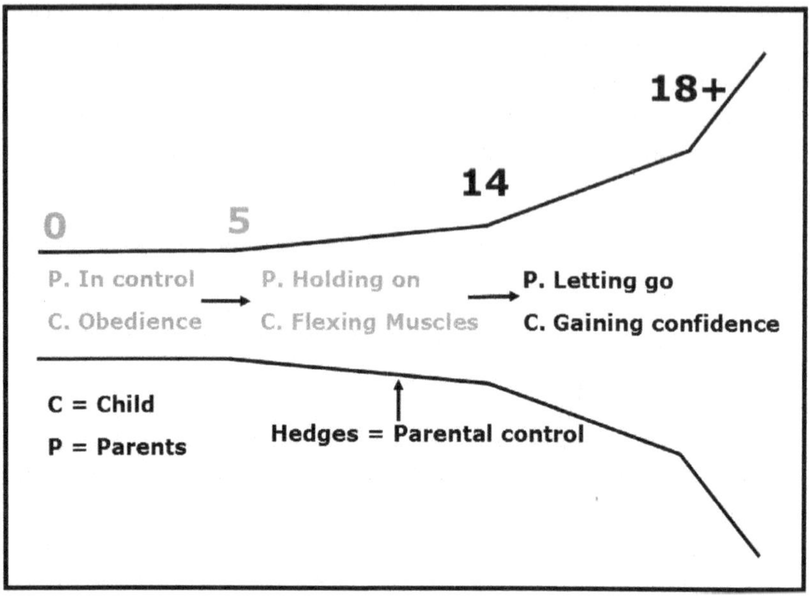

The lack of a fully connected prefrontal cortex means that our teenagers still need parental guidance and correction from us. They need us to hold on to them and not let them fully go until the time is right. They do not need a friend, they need parents; parents who will not let them go, and will do everything in their power to protect them from their lack of a fully connected prefrontal cortex. However, they are not young children anymore but emerging adults; the hedges may still be there; just wider apart.

The hedges are a barrier which says to our teenager, 'you can go so far but no further'. Take these hedges away and we are saying, 'You are capable of making sound judgments in all areas of your life', but this is effectively giving over complete control to our teenager who has a vital part of their brain not yet connected! The problem is that many of our teenagers think they are capable of taking complete control and so react when we keep the hedge in place. This is why clashes occur and why our teenager will often react with emotional outbursts.

The next chapter will deal with what the hedges are and how we can keep them in place.

Chapter 37

Hedges and teenagers

Hedges are still in place during the teen years and are the 'stop signs' through which you have helped to form 'neural pathways' in your child's brain. The hedges have also been helping to form your child's character and behaviour from birth until now. They are not physical or visible but psychological, as this quote from chapter 7 explains:

'We are the ones who set the hedges in place and we do not allow our child to stray outside of them. The difficulty is that our child cannot see the hedges because they are not visible. ... The hedges are in our mind; he or she can go here but not there, do that but not that. What we have to do is convince our child of it'. This concept is taken from the proverb, 'Train a child in the way he should go, and when he is old he will not turn from it'. (Proverbs 22:6)

All this has been taking place during childhood until this point in time. It is difficult to put new hedges in place during the teen years because it is those hedges that are already there that will be challenged and will hold up; or, if for a while they smash through the psychological hedges, the established 'neural pathways' will eventually bring them back in most cases. It is true that teenagers are quite capable of breaking away from your authority but it is not easy to break through the psychological authority that has been established over the whole of your child's life until now.

I was never a dad who just let my son win – he had to prove that he could win by his own merit and not just because I let him. Of course, there came a point where, physically, he could beat me every time having trained as a builder, but I played the psychological game and did everything I could to avoid taking on his physical challenge. In his mind, I was always the one to beat even though he was much stronger than I was. That was until the day when he was in his twenties when I foolishly accepted the challenge of an arm wrestle. Of course, he won easily, but it was his reaction that was interesting. He danced around the room celebrating that he had finally beaten me. The psychological barrier of my physical supremacy had been broken at last. In a similar way, you still hold parental authority and for your teenager's sense of security, you must not give up that authority.

What you have been trying to achieve throughout their lives up until this point continues. The goal is still adulthood; for our children to live successfully in this world, to build good relationships with others, to be well respected both socially and career-wise, and eventually, to have families of their own.

Teenagers are emerging adults who are at different stages of development during the last years of childhood. Thirteen to fifteen or even sixteen-year-olds would be expected to be still very much under parental discipline. Seventeen and eighteen-year-olds are right on the cusp of adulthood but as long as they are at school and under your care, are still subject to some parental discipline. Discipline is what hedges are about; using these hedges you are able to maintain and complete the character development of your teenager, and in doing so, keep your teenager safe and on track.

Discipline is the word that is used when a person is training for an athletic or academic task. An athlete who has entered for a marathon has to train under a coach's instruction or plan in order to achieve the goal. My daughter started running and wanted to enter a half-marathon. She started to build up her strength by gradually running greater distances until she felt she could finish the race. However, a problem arose because she did not feel she could do it because the more she ran, the worse she felt. Her legs ached, she felt tired and she thought she would never be able to do it. She mentioned this to a work colleague who ran full marathons, and he gave her a plan which involved doing a combination of short and long runs with rest periods. As a result, she successfully ran her first half-marathon in just over two hours.

This is what parental discipline is all about. It is the continued honing of our children's character skills – to respect people, to be honest and full of integrity, trustworthy, loyal to their principles and having a good work ethic. This began in the early years and is now in the last phase before adulthood is reached. We must continue to hold on until the prefrontal cortex is connected because teenagers are vulnerable to being thrown off course by peer pressure.

Referring to our previous diagram, the gaps between the hedges are much wider now and this means that our teenager has been given a lot more responsibility for their decisions and how they conduct their lives. For example, when my son went to secondary school he was given a measure of personal responsibility in that he was to travel to and from school on his own and to after-school activities. I, as his father, specifically gave over the responsibility for his actions when away from us, over to him. I told him that in effect he could do as he wished – it was his responsibility if he chose to swear, smoke or take drugs, steal or get involved with others who would lead him into things he knew I would disapprove of. I shared with him that not only could he choose but he would also have to accept the consequences of his choices. As a parent, I had to trust his character which had been developing under our training over the first eleven years of his life. As a parent I had no choice but to trust what we knew of his character, giving him the responsibility for his own actions. I decided to actually spell that out to him to make him think about it. As he got older he had to take more and more responsibility for his own actions but I was still there, still responsible, still the parent. The last hedge, apart from the common courtesies in relation to the people around him, was that he had to be in bed by ten o'clock on a school day.

As our children progress into their late teen years they need to take more and more personal responsibility for their actions when away from home. However, parental responsibility demands that if our teenager does decide to 'over-step the mark' and it comes to our notice, then we will need to exert our parental responsibility. It is no good pulling out the old saying, 'What you don't know can't hurt you' and ignoring the situation. For our teenager's well-being, there must be consequences for their behaviour.

Take the example of my young teen relative who was caught kicking and pulling down people's fences with a group of friends. He had broken through one of the hedges put in place by his parents; i.e. he had disrespected another people's property and was very rude to those who challenged him. What was the likely outcome of his parents doing nothing? It would most likely be repeat behaviour possibly leading to more serious incidents, and for this reason, there had to be consequences for breaking parental discipline.

Consequences can take many forms; loss of freedom, loss of allowances, extra chores – whatever affects your teenager most effectively. I remember on one of our first trips to New Zealand some young teenagers were caught smashing letterboxes with clubs. The police caught them and made them accompany them to every household and apologise. Their parents had to pay for replacement letter boxes, which I hope was then taken from their young teenagers' pocket money.

The question arises as to what these hedges are and how do they operate in the day-to-day life of a teenager?

As already outlined above, they are to do with the way they conduct themselves toward others. They are to do with respect, honesty, integrity and trustworthiness. If they have these character attributes then they are not going to go far wrong. The opposite attributes are that they are rude and disrespectful towards both people and property.

These are the lessons you have been trying to instil into your children from birth until now and you need to continue to insist that they continue to conduct themselves in this manner with those around them, including other family members. If you have insisted on these standards through the middle years they will already be a part of their personality and reminders are all that will be needed in the majority of incidents. If reminders do not work then other measures, such as being grounded or loss of pocket money, have to be taken. Teenager or not, there is still no excuse for rudeness.

Because their prefrontal cortex is not fully connected, we as parents still have to retain ultimate responsibility for our teenager's conduct even when we are not always with them. For your young person's sake do not, under any circumstances, abdicate that responsibility.

There are other areas where you may still have hedges in place and they could be things like doing chores around the home, and having earlier bedtimes during school term times. This doesn't mean that your teenager will respond well to this and there will always be some pushing against the hedges in their bid to be fully independent, but they are not yet quite ready so do not let them go just yet. I remember saying to my son, "The day will come when you will have to make your own decisions and decide which way you want to go, but this is not the time and until then I am not going to allow you to go in the wrong direction."

Always remember that teenagers need you, need to be with you and need to be participating in family times. A survey in Christchurch, New Zealand, indicated that fifty percent of all teenagers wanted to spend more time with their parents.

Three final points on parental hedges: The first is that they do have to get wider apart as your teenager is given more and more responsibility for their own life. However, there are limits; living within the law, respecting people and their property, respecting the family and extended family and the values you hold as a family – this includes setting a good example for younger members of the family. Most will do this naturally, but if they don't, you as parents need to pull them up and demand that as long as they live under your roof they need to conform to the values of the family culture. The truth is that most teenagers will do this if it has always been expected of them.

The second point is that you do have to let them go at some point. That point is usually when they finally leave school, start work or go to college.

Thirdly, always remember that you are still parents and that your children will always be your children. In fact your children, even in adulthood, need you to be parents, even when they act as if they do not. They do not need you to abdicate that role and they do not need you as friends. You are an anchor for them, somebody who is always there and who loves them unconditionally. Your attitude must gradually change through the teen years from being an authority figure to an advocate and advisor. My adult children ring us up and bounce things off us from time to time to get a different perspective on what is challenging them. Our attitude is, 'What do you think about this?' or, 'Have you thought about the consequences if you do that?' We suggest rather than instruct; we point out possible alternatives and obstacles rather than demand a certain action. We then encourage them to make their own decisions and we respect whatever decision they make

Chapter 38

Maintaining Relationship

The temptation is to think that now your child is a teenager you are becoming increasingly, or indeed are, irrelevant in your child's life. Somehow the message comes across that your teenagers no longer need you. This is just not the case for the majority of teenagers. Some may want more freedom than is good for them, but this does not mean that they no longer need or want you involved in their lives. The truth is that you are very important in your child's life and will continue to be even when they have established themselves as adults and have left home.

However, there are ways in which you can create far more frustration than there need be.

In chapter seven titled 'Danger – frustrated young people!' we drew attention to the biblical instruction in Colossians 3:20, that instructs children to, 'obey your parents in everything for this pleases the Lord'. We pointed out that there is a danger in overbearing parents demanding blind obedience in everything because this can frustrate our young people into wanting to leave home as soon as possible. This is expressed in the next verse, 'Fathers, do not provoke your children, lest they become discouraged'. The term 'father' in its original language is a root word signifying 'a nourisher, protector and upholder'. Our teenagers still need to be nourished, protected and upheld, but do not need to be held down so much that they lose their initiative, passion and drive for life.

When we lived in London we decided to spend the weekend with friends in Birmingham which was 192 km away. Our son, who was about 17 years old at the time, wanted to cycle while we went by car. Looking back, this was a foolish thing to do, but at the time we didn't think anything of it. Remember; there were no mobile phones in those days and we were on a motorway so even phone boxes were of no use. It was getting late and he still had not arrived, and we were getting worried. We went back along the route we knew he was taking and eventually found him quite close to

Birmingham. We were extremely relieved and he was very pleased as he was exhausted and happy for a lift home. However, it was important that we gave him the freedom to 'give it a go' and to let him decide even then whether we picked him up or he finished the ride himself. Young people need adventure, and even risk, from time to time but the important thing was that he knew we would be there for him if he needed us.

Another time he wanted to ride home from a Bible week at Plumpton Race Course – this was about 80km. However, that time we had a call from the hospital saying could we come and collect him. He was powering up a hill, looked up and saw nobody was in front of him so put his head down and went for it. Unbeknown to him a car had pulled in and parked. You can guess the rest. Imagine how frustrating it would have been for him if we had stifled any initiative, exploration or risk that he wanted to take. These same words can be applied in many other day-to-day aspects of a teenager's life.

It is essential that we maintain a relationship without stifling initiative, exploration or risk taking. How do we do this without endangering them?

There are four aspects we should consider; law, negotiation, consequences and trust.

1. Law

Compliance with the law of the land in which we live is non-negotiable. For us and those in our care, it is essential that we understand that non-compliance with the law can have serious consequences, and not just because we may be fined or even spend time in jail. A conviction can stop us visiting or living in certain countries and it can also make it very difficult for us getting certain jobs or pursuing certain careers. Some young people think that this does not matter, but the trouble is that it can come back to bite later in life. We see examples of this on reality television shows which features people entering certain countries. For example, a young man is trying to visit a country but has convictions in his youth. He is interviewed and in more cases than not is sent back home on the next available flight. It is our job as parents to do all we can to protect our children by stopping them getting into trouble with the law.

How can we do this? We do this by negotiation.

2. Negotiation

Let your teenager be a part of the decision making when they are seeking your advice or permission to do something. Don't be too hasty to say, 'no' but ask questions such as:

> "Who are you doing this with?"
>
> "How long do you anticipate it to take?"
>
> "What time will you be back?"
>
> "What are the risks and if there are risks, how are you going to handle them?"
>
> "Are you sure you can manage that?"
>
> "What will you do if this happens?"
>
> "What will you do in an emergency?"

Make sure it is age appropriate and be reluctant to say 'no'; if you do have to say 'no' make your reasons clear. This particularly applies when they are going out with others who you know are not trustworthy and are likely to get into some sort of trouble. If you feel for any reason they are in danger of getting on the wrong side of the law you must ask them questions like, "Your friend T. seems to be getting into trouble a lot lately; do you think it is a good idea to be getting involved with him/her so much?" "Your friends are going to be out until very late and I am not happy for you to be out at that time, do you think it is good for you to be out that late?"

3. Consequences

'What are the consequences and are you willing to accept them?' is a valid question; it makes our young people think not only about what they are about to do but what could happen as a result. If we encourage our teenager to consider the consequences, it doesn't mean that it is a 'no' but teaches our teenager to approach the situation with their eyes wide open so they can mitigate any risks they see, which is always a wise thing to do.

4. Trust

When you have negotiated and come to some decision with our teenager, then we can give them permission to go ahead. The fourth aspect is trust.

There are three relevant definitions of trust:

- The belief that you can trust someone or something
- A relationship based on trust and understanding
- To believe that something is true although you have no proof

You can choose to trust your teenager or decide otherwise. However, if you have no reason not to trust, then why not?

It is important to maintain your relationship with your teenager by allowing them to participate in some of the decisions that concern their lives. Having done that, it is a good thing to tell your teenager that you trust them.

The tools that you have used in bringing your teenagers up until to this point include love, praise, encouragement, understanding and actively listening to them. It does not mean these have changed or cease to be relevant; the truth is that they are still vital during the teen years.

Take love for instance – do you feel that this doesn't matter, now that your love for them is established? Oh course, not. Teenagers are vulnerable and often insecure, and need to know the security of your love for them.

What about praise, encouragement, understanding? Your approval, encouragement and belief in your teenager are vital for their well-being during these years. Do not be fooled; your teenager needs you to be on their side cheering them on as they march toward maturity. They also need the security of knowing you will protect them even when they don't appear to want it.

They need you to be parents, not friends. You are the ones that have always been their protector, security, provider and counsellor. It is a scary thing to face the adult world and all is changing; final exams are around the corner, university, career paths. Your teenagers need you, they need your encouragement, your praise and understanding as well as knowing you will continue to hold them to the path you have laid down. They need to do stuff with you, they need family fun, to feel special, wanted and that they matter.

Chapter 39

Personal responsibility

During the teen years, our teenager needs to gradually take responsibility for themselves where they can. This includes making decisions about what is important to them and how they will portion out their resources to meet their day-to-day lifestyle. Money, of course, is the key to most of what they want to do or be involved in. We, as adults, have certain resources which come to us through work, saving and investment. For all of us, there are limitations and we have to decide how to use those limited resources. We have to decide how much to put aside for all the essentials like rent/mortgage, gas/electricity, insurance, petrol and pleasure, to name a few. This is what being a responsible adult entails. There are those who do not do this and end up in terrible debt, and this debt can be very overwhelming.

Our teenagers are in the last phase of their training in becoming responsible adults who are able to take their place in the world, and eventually having their own careers, families and households. They need to continue to learn how to handle the limited resources they have, without always being bailed out by parents. To achieve this, you will need to expect your teenager to manage the resources and money available to them from their early teens. They need to make decisions on how they will use their money; what will it be used for, how much to spend and how much to put aside for future use. Being responsible for their own finances is a crucial step to becoming an adult. If they have been required to set aside money to spend, save and give in their middle years, then hopefully good principles and practices will have been established by the teen years. They must become responsible themselves for how they handle their personal resources and then accept the consequences, whether good or bad.

Of course, their resources come firstly from you, so you have to decide what, if any, allowance you give them. This will depend on what they can generate for themselves through paid jobs and chores they may do to earn extra cash. Discuss this with your teenager and negotiate, considering all angles both from your and their point of view. You will also need to consider those monies they may be earning from any jobs they may have. When one of my granddaughters got a job where her father worked, she paid for most of her needs from her wages and so her parents stopped most of their allowance to her. She then had to make her own decisions as to how she budgeted her earnings.

Be realistic about how much allowance you give but do not be so generous that your teenager has no need to budget or consider what they are spending their money on. For example, consider their mobile phones. What kind of phone and plan do they use and who is paying for it? Is it a smartphone with full data package giving full access to the Internet or is it a basic phone allowing just texts with a limited number of minutes for calls? Are you going to provide this or are you expecting them to pay for this out of their allowance? Our fifteen-year-old granddaughter was given an iPhone from a family friend and had to decide what package to buy, because even though she had WIFI at home, she had to pay for the plan out of her allowance herself. All good training for when she has left home and is independent.

Another example is clothes. Keeping up with the latest fashion trends can be expensive; when you are not paying for something, the sky is the limit with little consideration of cost. Give the responsibility over to your teenagers. Give them a clothing allowance which is in keeping with your own income and encourage them to hunt out bargains. Try not to make it too easy, even if your own resources are good, because they need to learn how to budget – when they go off to university or start work their resources will potentially not be great. It may be wise to keep such an allowance separate and require that it is only spent on clothes. School clothes, shoes and possibly underwear can be separate and still provided by you.

Wanting to get a loan is another thing that comes up from time to time. Your teenager may want a new mountain bike and either asks for it for birthday or Christmas or requests a loan to buy it. This poses several problems for parents – one being affordability on the parents' part, and another the ability of your teenager to repay the loan. This is, of course, the major consideration when a bank issues a loan. I remember when my son was a teenager; he wanted a new bicycle but there was no way we could afford it, and we had to consider his sister as well. Like most parents, we wanted to help out and knew that a new bike would be good for him. Our solution was to give what we could afford, and then get him to earn the rest. So, we gave him a combined Christmas/birthday present and he raised the rest of the money by doing extra jobs and saving his allowance. He was able to purchase the bike and it meant so much more to him because he had had to put some effort into obtaining it as well.

When you take out a loan you have to know you can repay it and so does the person giving the loan. You then have to sign an agreement that establishes a repayment plan. If you do not stick to that plan there are penalties. These usually take the form of interest added to the principal sum. If you continue to fail in making repayments, not only does the interest continue to rise but the lender will, in the end, repossess the object you took the loan for. If your teenager asks for a loan for a new bike or another item, consider whether you should set up an agreement with them, as to how it is to be repaid? Should there be penalties if repayments are not made? All this should be agreed upon before you give the loan; otherwise, no lessons will be learnt. Because it is family you might not charge interest or sign an agreement, but both of you should understand and accept the family agreement you have made.

We as parents want to be generous to our children but we must always consider whether it is good for their development when everything is provided 'on a plate'. We need to establish a balance between generosity and personal responsibility. The objective is not to make life difficult but to prepare them for life in an adult world.

I have heard of a family who charged their children for everything. They lived in a village and every time their teenagers wanted a lift somewhere a charge was made against their allowance. The same principles were used for clothes and anything the children wanted. When going to university the parents kept the student loans and any grants, divided it up and gave it in instalments as required. While I think they were trying to teach their children about the financial ways of the world, the potential truth was that it was possible they just made their children resent them and this created a barrier between them and their children. This is not what we want to achieve. Heathy families support each other with generosity and love, and prepare their teenager for adult life in ways which are gentle and kind, but not indulgent.

Do not make it too easy for your children, yet do not make it too hard either. Seek to strike a balance, keeping one eye on the values that underpin your actions and the other on a generosity of spirit. We train our teenagers to be like us, to assimilate our values and practices in the hope that it will hold them in good stead for their future life as adults.

Chapter 40

You must let go

Throughout this book I have tried to encourage you to train your child to take personal responsibility whenever possible. This begins at a very young age and continues until there comes a point when your child takes on the full responsibility for their own lives as they approach adulthood. In an ideal world, this would be progressive; starting with small, almost inconsequential steps like choosing which clothes to wear to ending with having to decide almost everything for themselves. This decision-making includes the areas of self-control and judging what to be involved in. For example, your child will at some point be confronted with behaviours which have harmful ramifications and they will have to decide whether to participate or walk away. The ability to do so depends on how, as a child, they have been encouraged and helped to assess the consequences of their actions. The 'law of consequences' helps us understand the outcomes of our decisions. Even though the prefrontal cortex is not yet fully connected up in the teenage brain and situations requiring judgements based on logic or assessing danger are not all they should be, if we have made it our habit to encourage our children to talk about, assess and think about the consequences of their actions right through childhood and up in to teen years, the odds are good that those lessons will not be completely forgotten.

Part of your end plan and goal should be to let your child go when they reach adulthood. For most parents that is scary! Nevertheless, that has to be the objective. Why? Because that is the eventual reality whether you like it or not. As I have been writing this I am very conscious that my son lives on the other side of the world and has become completely independent of us his parents. He has three daughters, all of whom are either away from home at university or working. Our daughter also has her own life and even though she lives in the same city, is in no way dependent on us, her parents. We have never tried to hold on to them, manipulate them, or seek to have life revolve around us. However, on the other hand, we love each other very much and we will talk and consult with each other on matters which arise in our lives. We are family and we will always maintain that relationship.

Many do not have such a relationship with their adult children and there are many reasons why this is. One of the reasons is that parents have tried to hold on too long because they fear for the future of their child, or they have sought to manipulate the relationship for their own benefit, not their children's benefit. As parents, our focus must be on our children for their sake, not ours. You cannot afford to have the attitude that you have given to them all these years and now it is time for them to repay you. Our job is to release them but at the same time letting them know they can return if necessary. This means that while they are finding their feet they have that security knowing parents and home are still there if they need to touch base, or come home for some reflection, peace or recuperation.

Some teenagers do not leave home when they have left school and do not go away to university. Some even come back after university and live at home for a while. Our children chose not to go to university, (one went later at the age of thirty), and both stayed at home until they were married. This was their choice, and for us, it was extra time with them before they married and had their own families. We all got on well with no particular conflicts so life was not difficult with them staying at home. We always understood that it was their home as well as ours – we had brought them into this world and they were a part of us as long as they wanted to remain with us. However, if there had been traumatic conflicts of lifestyle, then a time would have had to come when it would have been better for them to leave home and find their own way. For our children living at home was always going to be temporary; there was always going to come a time when they established their own home and life.

One family I know packed up their daughter's room when she left for university and gave it to her brother. There was no offer of her using her brother's old room if she wanted to return. She no longer had a base at home and, as I understand it, was deeply shocked and hurt, so much so that she apparently does not want to go home anymore. I find that harsh and hurtful as it had been her room her whole childhood and now, not only had her room been taken away but even her brother's old room was not made available to her. The message the parents gave was, 'You are no longer a part of this family and this is no longer your home'. Even if that was not the intention that undoubtedly was the message received. As a consequence, that young lady is now very vulnerable.

There does come a time when children no longer have a room which is theirs back at home. This can be when they have bought their own house or flat or most likely when they marry and set up home with a partner. However, there is a big difference between letting them go and cutting them off from everything they know. Let the leaving happen naturally; otherwise, you are in danger of giving out the wrong message.

There are, of course, some parents who have no choice other than to give their children notice that they are loved but no longer welcome to live at home. When disruptive behaviour, recklessness and lack of respect have become so severe, that life for parents and child has become intolerable, and if the child is of age, then sometimes that is the way it has to be. In this situation, parents should ask their child to leave, making sure they understand that it is not for lack of love, but necessary because of the future well-being of all concerned.

Think of it this way; your child has known nothing else – this is where they have always belonged. This is where their security has always been and it is a scary thing to be thrust into the world with no fall back or anchor. It is one thing to want to expand horizons by travelling or getting your own place; it is another to have no home base where you are not only accepted for who you are, but always welcome. That gives a sense of security and well-being; an anchor even while you are finding your way in this world.

Young people can feel very vulnerable, insecure and lost while trying to establish themselves in the world because they have not only physically and mentally left home but left home emotionally as well.

Letting go is not being cut off.

Chapter 41

The teenager's perspective

I sat at my desk thinking about what else I could write about teenagers and wrote on my reminder pad, 'Talk to the teenagers themselves'. I was not at all sure how viable this was so left it for a while but continued contemplating the possibility. I then had coffee with a perceptive friend who, without being prompted, advised me to get the young people together, buy them McDonald's and find out how they felt about being a young person in today's world. This was the prompt I needed so I arranged to visit our church's youth group, TKY – The Kings Youth.

Not being sure how to go about this I prepared some questions to prompt discussion and gave the teenagers post-it notes to write their individual responses to each other's perspectives and to my questions – green for approval, red for disapproval and yellow for undecided. Before I had even begun to ask any questions, a discussion developed around the difference between a thirteen to fifteen-year-old and a sixteen to seventeen-year-old. The teenagers pointed out that even though these ages were not that far apart, they felt that there was a huge difference when looking at things like rights, privileges, and personal responsibilities. They stressed the point that during the early teen years parents still needed to exert oversight but also needed to trust their teenager to take responsibility for themselves in some areas. However, they felt that when a young person reached the sixteen/seventeen mark there should be much more freedom and personal responsibility. There was even some discussion that there was a significant gap between the ages of sixteen and seventeen. As we shall see there was much discussion on how far the parental 'stops' should go. Parents, they felt, should trust the older teenagers even though that trust was not without limits.

The teenagers stated that they wanted to be a part of family life and wanted to relate to their parents, but they also wanted to be trusted to make good decisions for themselves. However, as we shall see, they still had a deep understanding of parental responsibilities and did not want to be given total independence. Parents were still, and would remain, important throughout their lives.

The first question I asked for comment on was:

What are parents responsible for?

The young people had a good understanding of their parent's responsibilities acknowledging that it gave them a strong element of safety as emerging adults – almost like there was a safety net that protected them.

The first list deals with the parent's general care of their child:

- Feeding, clothing and giving a roof
- Keeping me fed and clothed until you can get a job
- For big stuff at school
- Healthcare – doctor's appointment, dentist, medication

When it came to others putting a green, red or yellow dot against each comment to agree, disagree or indicate uncertainty, the majority were green with just a few indicating uncertainty around healthcare.

The second list seems to go a little deeper in the understanding of the parent's role:

- Keeping myself accountable and enabling (me to be) open to growth
- Encouragement and fostering strengths
- Being an example of how they want us to live, but still given space to try new things
- Caring for their kid's emotions – trying to understand their kid's emotions, encouraging their kids to be the best form of themselves (while) accepting their child for who they are
- Setting examples

Here the young people seem to be expressing a need for empathy, a deep understanding of their emotional needs and acceptance but without condemnation. The secret of an empathetic person is being able to not only identify where people are at, but to also be able to reach out to the emotion being expressed, without giving the impression of condemnation, acceptance or approval. All of these received green dots of agreement from others in the group. A teenager's first response is emotional, so any emotion cannot be ignored.

The third list indicates a need to feel safe and not abandoned:

- Keeping you safe
- My safety, social aspects and development, what we watch
- Where you are, e.g. friend's parties – have a curfew
  (This is very much age-related; some strong discussion regarding age here)
- Well-being, emotionally, physically

The responses given for the question, 'What are parents responsible for?' suggested that the young people still wanted their parents' involvement in their lives but not heavy-handed control nor domination over every aspect of their lives; rather an empathetic relationship that guarded, guided and directed through love, and did not ignore emotional reactions but rather sought to understand them. In an atmosphere like this young people know that there is a 'stop' and will accept that if they know they have been listened to, even though they may not agree with the 'stop'.

The second question was: What should you be responsible for?

- Obeying your parents, (concentrating on) your education
- Fostering and setting your own goals, selecting your own interests
- Making smart decisions – respecting your parents, your education, striving to excel in life; talking to your parents if needed
- Seeking help when needed; teenagers are really good at hiding how we feel and we need to learn how to ask for help
- Parents should conduct a healthy relationship
- Spiritual well-being, continuing to develop the good things your parents fostered when you were younger, education, good eating, TV etc
- Keeping yourself safe, being responsible
- What we want to have as a job and money decisions

These answers showed that the teenagers understood the need to take personal responsibility while accepting that parents were needed to support, care and keep them safe. There was an acknowledgement that teenagers are not good at seeking help, but that it did help if their parents were seen to be working on maintaining a healthy relationship with them. That, of course, is a two-way street – to be successful both parents and teenagers need to work on their relationships.

There was one other comment under this heading which caused quite a bit of discussion and disagreement. This came up when we were discussing the parental task of keeping teenagers safe. The comment was; 'Who our friends are'. In other words, do parents have the right to 'interfere' or 'put limits' on who their friends are? Some felt a definite no – these tended to be the older ones, who were seventeen plus. Others felt that part of keeping them safe was keeping them safe from influences that would corrupt them and put them in danger. They talked about those who were taking drugs, drinking excessively and late-night partying. The discussion was inconclusive but they were aware of the potential problems and influences that friends could have. There seemed to me to be an underlying desire for parents to be that 'back-stop' that kept them safe, especially among the younger teenagers.

The next question was: How much do you need your parents?

- As a teenager – (you) feel parents know nothing; as an adult – you realise what they do know and that they have been there themselves
- Brick wall – do not always realised how much as a teenager, we need the limits which parents give
- As a guide more than a harsh authority
- Need parents to communicate well
- Need parents to try to understand and listen
- Recognise that it is hard for parents as well as teenagers

There is no doubt at all that most young people need and want their parents in their lives. What they do not want is to be shut out, their views not heard and for them to feel dismissed. A major need is to be listened to without preconceived reactions from parents. One young person said,

"Technically, for survival, we don't 'need' them. But for full growth and flourishment you need them for your whole life."

Finally, I asked them what they would like to say to parents – the answers were brief and to the point:

- Teenagers can be dumb but (they) don't think they are.

We know, and so do young people, that sometimes teenagers do dumb things, but they do not think they do until afterwards. This means that to relate to young people successfully, they said we need to 'be empathetic'. This is having the ability to understand and share the feelings of another. For example, 'she's compassionate and empathetic towards her daughter'. If you are to be empathetic you are always trying to understand others and are compassionate rather than judgemental. As the next quote from the young people says: 'Be at their level'.

- If we are to achieve this we need to 'listen and hear'.

It is so easy to listen without really hearing and in order to achieve this, we need to put aside all preconceived, ready-made responses, make eye contact and ask questions until we think we understand. When you think you understand, ask the question, "Is this what you are saying?" and repeat back what it is you think you heard. If you have got it wrong repeat the process until you truly understand and then you can negotiate, object, say 'no' or give approval. You might still have a fight on your hands if it goes against the teenager's viewpoint, but you will be amazed at the mutual respect you will find, even while disagreeing.

This chapter has been read by all the young people involved in the discussion; corrections have been made and all are in general agreement with what I have recorded.

Chapter 42

A teenager's perspective

One of our teaching series at church was entitled *Living life well* and one of the speakers was nineteen-year-old Charlotte who spoke about what it was like to be a teenager in today's society. As I listened I realised that she had some very important things to say, and so I have asked her to write a chapter for me. Here it is and I recommend it wholeheartedly.

At the ripe old age of 19, standing on the precipice of adulthood, I can say with confidence that I have enjoyed being a teenager. Adulthood leads to responsibility, difficult life choices and exorbitant bus fares. But I can also say with conviction that being a teenager is difficult. Every generation says that they had it the toughest like it's a badge of honour to have a particularly rough adolescence. Whenever a teenager begins to complain about growing up, they are bombarded with stories about 'back in my day' when students had to walk to school, in the snow, without shoes, fearing nuclear war. I cannot claim that my generation has taken the cake for the worst youth ever; I am sure all teenagers throughout history have experienced similar struggles. But the conditions of contemporary society have somewhat transformed and/or intensified these problems, while creating new struggles for teenagers to face, just for good measure. I am no teenage guru. I cannot definitively state the single reason that teenagers are struggling in the 21st century. All I can do is share my experience of growing up and hope there is something valuable amongst my many tangents.

Big brother is watching you. And your parents, teachers, friends and Instagram followers are watching too. For thirteen years you are constantly surrounded by people. Your actions are watched by your teachers, classmates and parents. You are continually tested and graded both academically and socially. Even when you get home, social media ensures that you are never really disconnected. The most awkward stage of your life is under a microscope and can be immortalised on your

Facebook timeline. While being watched, you are given a label; a summation of who you are. It could be smart, sporty, popular, stupid, a nerd or a bad kid. And when you get a label you either do everything you can to get rid of it, at the expense of who you really are, or constantly try and live up to it.

For me, my worth came from how hard I worked. If I received a slightly disappointing grade, it felt like the world was coming to an end. It didn't matter that this was a Year 10 social studies assessment on the history and geography of Southeast Asia that had zero impact on my future (just a completely random example). When it seems like your life is under a microscope, every disappointment feels magnified. Nothing made me want to hit someone more than the phrase, 'you are only _____ years old, this test doesn't even matter'. Surprisingly, the sudden revelation that all my hard work was for nothing didn't dissolve all the stress I had been feeling.

The pressure to succeed did not come from my parents. They have always been supportive of me and would rather that I be content with who I am than a top student at Cambridge University (both equally challenging). But when you add social media and an assessment-focussed education system to the mix, the pressure to succeed ensues. And this can lead to an inability to fail. Growing up should be a time for spectacular failures creating valuable life lessons to tell the grandkids. But unfortunately, there is now an institutionalised fear of failure.

From a relatively young age, I was thinking about the future. I needed to get good grades at school, balanced with enough extra-curricular activities to seem well-rounded. This could lead to a scholarship paying for my university degree, allowing me to a get a good job. To get a job, I would need perfect grades, 100 years of experience and to be Mother Teresa in my spare time. Finally, if I worked hard maybe I could eventually enter the particularly difficult housing market. This would ensure stability in my old age, especially as the age of retirement will be 120 by the time I am eligible. Therefore, failing that Year 10 social studies project could potentially lead to homelessness and destitution so don't tell me not to panic! Maybe this is a slight exaggeration, but it is not an exaggeration to say that many of my friends feel anxious about the future. We hear about how difficult it is to get jobs, how tough the housing market is, the rate of child poverty and homelessness and it somewhat crushes our youthful optimism. Not every teenager is like this, but I would say a significant proportion of my generation has this perspective of the future. In my first semester at university, my lecturer had to spend half a lesson telling my class to relax. She described us as the highest achievers, and yet the most anxious students she had ever taught. When talking about the problems of youth, we focus on drinking, drugs and social media; placing the problem and the blame back on youth. But too often the more complicated situations are overlooked. It is more difficult to discuss the crippling fear of failure in a highly competitive neoliberal society than the evils of alcohol.

Basically, my ramblings can be summarised as follows – teenagers have a loss of perspective. On our identity, the gravity of our mistakes and the future we are entering into. When it feels like everyone is watching you, it is easy for your identity to be wrapped up in performance. When it seems your failures are seen by everyone, in a society where failure is not tolerated, any mistake you make is the end of the world. And when your perspective of the future is of fear and uncertainty, it is hard not to feel anxious in the present. This is not the holy grail of teenagers' problems. This is just the ramblings of a girl whose only source of authority to discuss teenagers is that she is one. But I am cheaper than a psychiatrist and with the amount of money you have to spend on the bus, you need all the savings you can get.

Fortunately, not all of my youthful optimism has been knocked out of me (yet). I really enjoyed my time at school and think that growing up doesn't have to be so hard. And it all starts with a ground-breaking phenomenon that I like to call communication. Ah yes, communication. The buzzword in all relationship-based literature available in a bookstore near you. But I genuinely believe that better communication between teenagers and adults would go a long way. Parents; I know that you believe teenagers cannot muster more than a grunt or shrug when talking to an adult, but I believe that miracles can happen. From a very young age, my parents made time to talk about how my day was. On the drive home from school, I would explain every detail of the day while my mum patiently nodded and laughed at the right moments. When I grew older, the tradition continued and still does to this day. Teenagers; I know you believe your parents were born as 30-year-old adults and can't possibly understand. But, surprisingly, every parent has been a teenager and come out the other side. They also have had their struggles and disappointments but know that school is a small fraction of a person's life. They can talk about the mistakes they've made but also, in a Christian family, explain how God has supported them in every hurdle. Parents can help teenagers regain perspective. Of course, this also means that teenagers have to listen to their parents, which may require a bit more than a miracle!

This communication should extend beyond the relationships between parents and children. There is a breakdown in communication between the older and younger generation. It seems that adults genuinely want to help and support the youth of their city, but forget to actually consult said youth. I recently went to a workshop discussing how to engage with youth and equip them for the future. In the room was myself, one other young person and a group of adults. What proceeded was a 15-minute discussion on how youth don't want responsibility, how we are lazy, how we are like an indigenous minority (my particular favourite) and all sorts of condescending pearls of wisdom. I watched as the other young girl tried to interject and provide the youth's perspective. But every time she tried to speak, someone would interrupt her. This happened four or five times until she finally managed to talk over the top of everyone. After she had said the most sensible thing I had heard during the whole workshop, the adults decided to ignore her point and go back to their previous conversation. What they didn't realise was that this girl was the chairperson of an organisation trying to prevent bullying and the abuse of social media among youth. In fact, last year she had met the Queen to receive the New Zealand's Queen's Young Leader Award. If anyone knew how to engage with youth, it was her. But in their passion, the adults in the room had inadvertently alienated the people they were trying to help. While adults' advice and experiences are very beneficial, the main thing teenagers want is to be heard. And until young people feel like their perspective is genuinely valued, we cannot move forward.

Growing up is always going to have its hurdles. Navigating relationships, school and bad skin days are never going to be a smooth ride. But the issues of identity, failure and the future are problems that teenagers cannot handle alone. We need people who have lived longer and have had more experience to put our situations in perspective. We need 'back in my day' stories to show that failure isn't the end. And we just need people to have honest conversations with us about how we are feeling. If we are properly equipped to fight the beast of adolescence, then we will be able to provide proper support for the next generation. A wise philosopher, W. E. Houston, once said, "I believe the children are our future, teach them well and let them lead the way." And I couldn't agree more.

Chapter 43

Final thoughts

Of all the things I have written on parenting, writing about teenagers has been the hardest to pin down. They are all so different and because of this, it is quite difficult to be definite and specific about how to go about the task of guiding them through these last years of their development into adult life.

When I was thinking about how to finish the teenager's part of this book, I came across a blog by Christie Halverson[20]. (1) She says that when asked what the secret to raising great teenagers is, her first reaction is to say that she has no clue. I agree with that reaction because that is what it feels like after watching our own children, grandchildren and their friends go through teen years and become great adults, husbands, wives and parents. 'Just how did that happen?' we ask ourselves. After this initial thought and musing on it for a while we realised that it was not the teen years that determined the outcome, but the years that have gone before; and particularly the first five years that shaped what our child, teenager and then adult would become. I would agree with Christie that the first thing necessary is 'to disbelieve the myth that teenagers are sullen, angry creatures who slam doors and hate their parents'. Some do that but the vast majority of them do not. Very few teenagers I have known have been like that and Christie says that her children and their friends have also not been like that. Teenagers want to be, indeed need to be, validated, loved and fed a lot!

Christie shared seven 'rules' for raising great teenagers. I have adapted them for this book but the ideas are hers. Rules? Yes, not for them but for you. Rules are the last thing your teenagers need. However, we need to understand that there are things that we do which either frustrate or

---

20 http://stiesthoughts.com/stiesthoughts/2014/5/7/55zvwekavna2c2md9q5j4ezya55j8q May 2018

release them, and yet at the same time, it is still our responsibility to keep them safe and secure in their topsy-turvy world.

1. Love them fiercely

Love everything about them; yes, even the annoying things. Love them in their actions and their intentions. Actively let them know just how much you love them by not being overcritical of their scruffy dress, untidy rooms, procrastination or scattered brains. Realise that what is happening to them is a miracle of transformation – from sometimes annoying teenager to a responsible adult, loving future partner and parent. Their prefrontal cortex has not yet fully connected, resulting in them not often showing much responsible action. Love them anyway; see them as a privilege to raise, and not as a burden. They are more perceptive than you can imagine; how you feel about them will be no secret to them, so just love them.

2. Listen and pay attention

When they walk through the door after school, you have a few precious minutes when they will divulge the secrets of their day with you. Be excited to see them, put down the cell phone and stop what you are doing. Do not waste a moment of this time by being distracted. Look them in the eye and be excited to see them and listen to what they have to say. Make their victories your victories. Be empathetic when things have gone wrong, reach out and touch them letting them know you have heard what they say. Don't offer advice or lecture during this time unless they ask for it. Just listen – it makes them feel important and valued. This is your time to focus on them, listen to what they are saying and feeling right then and there; don't allow yourself to be distracted. This moment may not last long; make the most of every second. It is really hard to navigate middle school and high school, and they need you as their secure unmovable platform, their safe place which they can always come back to after negotiating life when away from you. Do not for one moment believe that they do not need you. A youth specialist recently said that the one thing young people desperately want and need today is more time with their parents.

3. Say 'yes' more than 'no'

'The world is forever going to tell them no. For the rest of their lives, they will be swimming in a stormy sea with wave-after-wave of 'you're not good enough' and 'you can't do this' crashing down on their heads. If nothing else, I want to be the opposite voice in their lives for as long as I can. I want to instil in them the belief that they are not limited, and that they can do anything if they're willing to work hard enough for it. I want to be the 'yes you can' in their life. I want them to leave my house every day feeling invincible'. (Christie Halverson)

You can feel Christie's passion for her children and that will communicate itself to them. Imagine a world where everything is 'no'. What a negative image that conjures up, whereas a 'yes' creates a much more positive atmosphere and one thing teenagers need is positivity.

4. Say 'no' often

Once again quoting directly from Christie Halverson.

'You need to say 'no' to experiences and situations that will set your child up for harm or unhappiness. Don't let them go to the parties where they will be forced to make a choice at age sixteen in front of their peers about alcohol. Don't let them stay out until three in the morning with a member of the opposite sex. Be the parent. Set up rules for their safety, both physical and moral. You would think this rule goes without saying, but we have known a shockingly large number of parents who don't use it'.

There is a 'no' because it is part of our job to create a safe environment for these fledgeling adults. We will not let them go into situations where they will be in danger or damaged. Sometimes that will be difficult for them and you, but be careful with 'no' and prefer 'yes', but if in doubt make use of 'maybe'. Before using 'no' ask lots of questions which puts the emphasis on the teenager coming to their own conclusions.

Questions such as:

- Do you think it is wise to get involved there?
- What sort of problems do you think you will come up against if you do that or go there?
- How will you handle that if things get difficult?
- Can you trust so-and-so not to go too far?

When you have given your teenager time to talk and discuss some of these questions with you, then you may be able to come to a mutual agreement and the 'maybe' can become 'yes', but if not, only then use the 'no'. A lot of 'maybe's' will end up as 'no's' but in this way you will have allowed your teenager to be part of the discussion. However, if you just know that it is wrong, don't hold out false hope, it is simply 'no'; always let your 'no' have a clear explanation even if they do not agree with your conclusions.

5. Feed them a lot

'And not only them but their friends, too. These bodies are growing and developing at an astonishing rate, and need fuel to do so – most of which they prefer to be loaded with processed sugar and hydrogenated-something-or-other. When their friends know your pantry is stocked to the gills with treats, they will beg your kid to hang out at your place. This allows you to not only meet and know their friends but to keep an eye on your teenager as well. Make your house the fun house. Buy that ping-pong table. Get the newest gaming system. Put in a pool. Or a basketball hoop. Your return on investment will be greater than any other options out there'. (Christie Halverson)

6. Don't sweat the small stuff

Once again quoting Christie in full:

'Don't sweat the small stuff. When living with teenagers, it can be so easy to see the backpack dropped in the middle of the living room as laziness. Or the bedroom scattered with dirty clothes as irresponsible. Instead, and before you open your mouth to yell at them, put yourself in their shoes. Find out about their day first. Maybe they are feeling beaten down, and they just need to unwind for a minute and tell you about it. Maybe they're tired from all that growing, learning, working, and 'hormone-ing'. If you waste your chance and yell at them about the backpack or shoes or [insert every other possession they own], they will not open up to you. Breathe. Ignore it for a bit and put your arms around that big, sweaty kid and give him a hug. Talk to him about his world. Find out what he did, wants to do, and dreams of doing. Then, and only then, ask him to pick it up and put it away.

That being said, do I completely ignore the state of my boys' bedrooms all the time? No, I do not. But I pick my battles, and I pick the appropriate time to fight them. Once every seven to ten days or so, I tell them their bedrooms need to be picked up. Which they do happily because it's not the running loop of a nagging mom. They know when I ask, it needs to be done.

I will not have a bad relationship with my kid over a pile of clothes on the floor. It's not worth it. I love my kid more than I love a clean house. I am confident that I am raising humans capable of picking up after themselves, and I know as they mature and grow up, these things will sort themselves out. I have taught them how to do it. They will not be in college and literally unaware of how to bend down and pick up their socks'.

7. Stand back and watch the magic happen

'Last, but not least, is to stand back and watch the magic happen. If you let them, these glorious creatures will open their hearts and love you more fiercely than you could possibly imagine. They are brilliant, capable, strong spirits who bring with them a flurry of happiness. They are hilarious and clever. They are thoughtful and sensitive. They *want* us to adore them. They *need* us to adore them. They love deeply and are keenly in touch with the feelings of others.

They are just about the greatest gift that God gave to parents.

And I'm beyond lucky to call this crazy group mine'.

I love the passion and belief that comes through in Christie's blog and thought it well worthwhile quoting it. Above all, do not cease to pray for your children no matter what age they are. Our own children are fifty and forty-eight and we still pray for them almost daily, as we do for all five granddaughters. The simple fact is we love them, believe in them and are passionate that they will lead good godly lives and as long as we reside on this earth we will continue to do so. Eventually, their prefrontal cortex connects up and at that point, all that you have put into them is established and will remain.

'Train a child in the way he should go, and when he is old he will not turn from it'.

Proverbs 22:6

Appendix 1

Summary of the timeout method of correcting our children

1. Tell the child to stop.
2. If they continue to do what we have asked them to stop doing, warn them of the consequences of continuing. Say 'If you do that again you will go to timeout.' Do not send them to timeout without the warnings, otherwise you will confuse them.
3. If the child does it again, calmly pick him or her up and take them to the timeout spot, telling them clearly why. 'You disobeyed me; you must do as you are told'.
4. Time the timeout one minute for every year of their age.
5. At the end of the timeout return and ask them why they were in time out. What you want to hear is, 'I did not do as I was told'. The point is not what they were doing but that they did not do as they were told.
6. Ask them to say sorry. Do not make a big drama out of it; even a begrudging sorry is fine.
7. End with big cuddles and even a bit of a tickle, and do not refer to the incident again.
8. Carry on as normal and if it happens again, go through it all over.

You may have your own way of making your 'no' mean no. We must make sure you are consistent and that you do not confuse the issue here which is obedience. Confusion is the enemy at this stage of life.